The Critical Circle

THE CRITICAL CIRCLE

Literature, History, and
Philosophical Hermeneutics

David Couzens Hoy

UNIVERSITY OF CALIFORNIA PRESS

Berkeley   Los Angeles   London

UNIVERSITY OF CALIFORNIA PRESS
BERKELEY AND LOS ANGELES, CALIFORNIA
UNIVERSITY OF CALIFORNIA PRESS, LTD.
LONDON, ENGLAND

ISBN: 0-520-03434-1
LIBRARY OF CONGRESS CATALOG CARD NUMBER: 76-52028

PRINTED IN THE UNITED STATES OF AMERICA

1 2 3 4 5 6 7 8 9 0

Contents

Foreword

The Critical Circle investigates the celebrated hermeneutic circle, especially as it manifests itself in historical inquiry and literary criticism. Formulated variously in different theories of hermeneutics, the circle generally describes how, in the process of understanding and interpretation, part and whole are related in a circular way: in order to understand the whole, it is necessary to understand the parts, while to understand the parts it is necessary to have some comprehension of the whole. Whereas in earlier hermeneutics the circle is used primarily to describe the understanding of texts, in the hermeneutic philosophy of Martin Heidegger and Hans-Georg Gadamer the circle becomes a fundamental principle of man's understanding of his own nature and situation. Understanding, and with it the hermeneutic circle, becomes a condition for the possibility of human experience and inquiry. The discovery and description of such conditions are the task of critical philosophy. The term "critical" in the title, then, suggests that the circle is not a merely adventitious feature of the criticism of literary texts. On the contrary, it is a category discovered by critical philosophy to be essential and indispensable to all humanistic thinking.

The term "critical" also connotes crisis, and indeed it is a theme of the phenomenological tradition, and of Heidegger and Edmund Husserl in particular, to insist that the natural and humanistic sciences face a crisis that requires philosophical reflection on their very foundations. Whether or not the humanities in general and the literary sciences in particular face such a crisis today is an open question. The present proliferation of interpretive methods provides some evidence that a crisis does exist. There is a general desire to rethink the very nature of literary interpretation, often accompanied by the hope of overcoming the crisis by making interpretation more objective and "scientific." But the hermeneutic circle cannot be the solution to such a crisis, since hermeneutic philosophy aims precisely to provoke reflection, and to challenge the putative certainty of established methods. Not a new method or "approach" to practical interpretation, the hermeneutical theory is more generally a prolegomenon to a philosophical poetics. Since poetry can only come to be in an understanding, the first step involves an account of the conditions for the possibility of the *understanding* of poetic works. According to the hermeneutic account, however, the understanding of a text is conditioned by the self-understanding of the interpretation. This means that the reflection on the ways in which the literary understanding has come about is a crucial moment of literary criticism. Self-reflection and a clearer self-understanding are critical if the interpretive process is to realize its essential possibilities.

Hermeneutic philosophy also emphasizes the extent to which self-understanding is conditioned by the tradition in which it stands and the continuing community of researchers to which it relates. The present study must likewise acknowledge its debts to a number of thinkers. Without the original inspiration of discussions with Karsten Harries and Hans-Georg Gadamer this book would not have been written. The manuscript owes much to criticisms and ideas from students at Yale, Princeton, and UCLA, as well as from such colleagues and friends as Richard Rorty, Stanley Corngold, Walter Kaufmann, Edward Casey, Richard Palmer, Peter McCormick, Werner Marx, Ludwig Siep, and the hospitable Kümmerers of Tübingen, Germany. My wife, Joyce Beck Hoy, has contributed immeasurably to both theoretical and practical aspects of the realization of this book. A portion of Chapter Five is published in Marie-Rose Logan's special issue of *Yale French Studies* (No. 52, 1975) on literature and philosophy. I am grateful to Robert Zachary for his patience and encouragement, and to Ruth Hein for her editorial assistance. Research for this book was generously supported by Princeton University and the Alexander von Humboldt-Stiftung.

Introduction

Though Hermes was known as the messenger of the gods, he did not necessarily always carry an explicit message, nor did his appearance invariably cause joy. His appearance itself could be the message—he was said to lead the souls into the underworld at death. So the Greeks knew a long time ago that the medium could be the message, but this insight did not breed the enthusiasm that it does today. In the *Cratylus,* for instance, Socrates points out that Hermes, the god who invented language and speech, could be called interpreter or messenger but also thief, liar, or contriver (see 408a-d). Words, Socrates says, have the power to reveal, but they also conceal; speech can signify all things, but it also turns things this way and that. Hence Socrates finds it significant that Pan, the son of Hermes, is smooth and divine above and goatlike below, for language itself is divided into the true and the false—the true insofar as it approaches the divine and the false insofar as it is associated with the tragic ways of man. Hermes himself was not above playing with this conflict, and hence the gods' messages were often oracular and ambiguous.

In the absence of Hermes, the modern age needs hermeneutics. In a more limited sense, hermeneutics is the concern with speech and writing, and hence with the methodology of interpretation of texts. When hermeneutics was largely an ancillary discipline of theology, the "word" to be interpreted was that of the Bible; interpretation involved spelling out the meaning of a word that already spoke to and claimed its hearers. Because such hermeneutics could presuppose the immediacy of the claim of meaning, it can be seen as essentially optimistic. Such optimism is radically undercut, however, by the suspicion that the surface clarity of conscious thought masks hidden struggles at deeper levels of consciousness. Such modern thinkers as Nietzsche, Marx, and Freud mark the rediscovery of the demonic side of Hermes.[1]

Subsequent hermeneutic theory is then charged with the task of describing the possibility of these new dimensions of interpretation, without necessarily falling into a reductivistic naturalism that explains the distortions of consciousness in terms of underlying physical or material causes. Hermeneutics becomes a philosophical problematic in its own right. The need is no longer the more restricted one of providing rules for proper interpretation; rather, a more encompassing necessity arises of explaining the conditions for the very possibility of understanding. Heidegger labels the philosophical project of *Being and Time* a hermeneutic phenomenology.[2] The term *hermeneutic* is not used restrictively to mean "the methodology of those humane sciences which are historiological in character" (*BT* 62; *SZ* 38). Heidegger believes this limited sense to be derivative from a more primordial philosophical "hermeneutics" that gives a philosophical interpretation of all human existence. Since philosophy is itself an aspect of human existence, the philosophical interpretation will also have to account for its own possibility. Such a philosophy will be hermeneutic in the further sense, then, of containing a circular reflection on its own conditions. In a passage that is now central to any discussion of hermeneutic, Heidegger discusses this hermeneutic circle:

Any interpretation which is to contribute understanding, must already have understood what is to be interpreted. This is a fact that has always been remarked, even if only in the area of derivative ways of understanding and interpretation, such as philological Interpretation. The latter belongs within the range of scientific knowledge. Such knowledge demands the rigor of a demonstration to provide grounds for it. In a scientific proof, we may not presuppose what it is our task to provide grounds for. But if interpretation must in any case already operate in that which is understood, and if it must draw its nurture from this, how is it to bring any scientific results to maturity without moving in a circle, especially if, moreover, the understanding which is presupposed still operates within our common information about man and the world? Yet according to the most elementary rules of logic, this *circle* is a *circulus vitiosus*. [*BT* 194; *SZ* 152]

Heidegger goes on to point out, however, that the circle is only vicious given a certain ideal of knowledge—the ideal of objectivity. Objectivity is not meant simply in the weak sense of "not purely subjective," nor in the moderate sense of "unbiased" or "disinterested." These senses often presuppose a much stronger sense in which scientific proof is said to be objective. The ideal in this stronger sense involves an epistemological model that has dominated the Cartesian tradition. It postulates the task of finding elements so fundamental that they cannot be further subdivided, using these simples as an incontestable starting point for rigorous deduction.

Not all human understanding has this kind of knowledge as its ideal, however. For instance, when the understanding takes place within a system of relations and consists of their detailed explication, there is nothing vicious about passing through the starting point again in the course of explication.[3] Heidegger maintains that such circularity underlies all understanding, and that the methodological ideal of scientific objectivism is merely derivative, appropriate only for a limited range of cognition:

> But if we see this circle as a vicious one and look out for ways of avoiding it, even if we just "sense" it as an inevitable imperfection, then the act of understanding has been misunderstood from the ground up.... What is decisive is not to get out of the circle but to come into it in the right way. This circle of understanding ...is not to be reduced to the level of a vicious circle, or even of a circle which is merely tolerated. In the circle is hidden a positive possibility of the most primordial kind of knowing. [*BT* 194-5; *SZ* 153]

In this discussion of the hermeneutic circle Heidegger has in mind the historical sciences (Geisteswissenschaften) rather than the natural sciences. He thinks it is a mistake, however, to denigrate the former and to insist on a radical difference in scientific rigor between them (*BT* 195; *SZ* 153). Historiography, in fact, is of special importance to Heidegger because it is the paradigm case for his attempt to push philosophical inquiry beyond the procedures of particular disciplines to the fundamental categories of all understanding and experience as such. The category he discovers in this case is that of historicity—the distinctive ontological mark of man, whose existence is always temporally and historically situated.[4] Historicity is an essential feature of the hermeneutical circle, and of philosophy as well. In contrast with the dream of Cartesian

"First Philosophy," on Heidegger's view there is no presuppositionless knowledge. All understanding presupposes a prior grasp,
a preunderstanding of the whole. Since preconceptions always
condition our knowledge, it is impossible to suppress every "subjective" determinant of understanding.

Heidegger's critique of the ideal of objectivity and his argument
for the primacy of a circular interpretive understanding awaken
fear of the ultimate dismissal of objectivity. Can scientists and
scholars any longer speak meaningfully of the truth or validity of
their conclusions? Can researchers engage in rational debate about
the appropriateness of methods, and can they appeal to "scientific" standards in the face of wild speculations?

Heidegger tries to allay these fears by granting some legitimacy
to objectifying research and by insisting that the preunderstandings that influence research and inquiry should not be based on
"fancies or popular convictions," but rather should be worked
out in terms of "the things themselves" (die Sachen selbst—*BT*
195; *SZ* 153). Heidegger himself only exploits the polemic value of
his critique, however, remaining cryptic about its positive consequences. Further analysis of the nature and procedure of the various humanistic and scientific disciplines is needed.

A more complete hermeneutic theory—one that devotes considerable discussion to the interpretive disciplines and yet incorpo-
rates Heidegger's account of understanding and the hermeneutic
circle—is provided by the Heidelberg philosopher and former student of Heidegger, Hans-Georg Gadamer.[5] Any student or scholar
of the humanities will want to know whether this new philosophical hermeneutics gives a reasonable description of the processes of
understanding and interpreting. For humanists, the central question concerns the grounds by which their interpretations can be
said to be valid and their insights true. Any hermeneutic theory
should account for the possibility of adjudicating between conflicting interpretive understandings. A theory unable to do so will
be called radical relativism and most probably dismissed as useless.
Whether Gadamer's philosophical hermeneutics can carry through
its critique of objectivism without falling into relativism will be the
central concern of this book.

Not all hermeneutic theorists follow the lines of Gadamer and
Heidegger, and this study begins by examining some recent objec-

tions to what is considered the dangerous historical relativism still lurking in Gadamer's philosophy. In the important book *Validity in Interpretation,*[6] E. D. Hirsch develops a very different herme- neutical answer from Gadamer's to the questions of the nature and locus of meaning in literary texts, and the validity of the inter- preter's understanding of such meaning. In contrast with the prin- ciples of the American New Criticism, Hirsch strives to guarantee the objectivity of interpretation by reviving the notion of the author's intention. Gadamer's and Heidegger's apparent histori- cism—their insistence on the historical conditions of knowledge and thought—would be undercut by this attempt at breaking out of the hermeneutical circle and anchoring the chain of interpreta- tion in the bedrock of the author's intention and the one right in- terpretation following from it. The sharp divergence between Gadamer and Hirsch on the methodology of interpretation is the result of the same fundamental disagreement about the nature of philosophy that led Heidegger to break with Husserl's more Car- tesian phenomenology and to label his own distinctively anti-Car- tesian philosophy a hermeneutical one. Hirsch combines a sym- pathy for Husserl with one for the more traditional line of herme- neutics running from Schleiermacher and Dilthey to the contem- porary Italian theorist, Emilio Betti.[7] Gadamer, on the other hand, follows Heidegger in abandoning the foundationalist enterprise that looks for a presuppositionless starting point in the self-cer- tainty of subjectivity, and in stressing instead the interpretive and historical character of all understanding, including philosophical self-understanding.

This difference becomes clear in the discussion of Hirsch's views about the intention and meaning of literary texts in Chapter One, which serves as a propaedeutic for the exposition of the basic con- cepts of Gadamer's philosophical hermeneutics in Chapter Two. Gadamer's most original contribution to the history of hermeneu- tics is his linguistic turn. In contrast with hermeneutic theories that view understanding as a psychological process mediating the pri- vate experiences of separate subjectivities (such as a writer and a reader), Gadamer thinks of understanding as a linguistic phenom- enon. Whereas previous hermeneutics may have appealed to a con- cept like empathy to close the gap between text and interpreter, Gadamer develops the idea of what he calls the linguisticality

(Sprachlichkeit) of understanding in order to eliminate the very problem of such a hermeneutical gap. Other recent philosophers in the Continental tradition have also advanced theories of the nature of writing (Jacques Derrida) and of the semantic dimensions of interpretation (Paul Ricoeur). In Chapter Three Gadamer's concept of linguisticality is tested both against these theories and against the special problems presented by the self-conscious linguisticality of literary texts.

Gadamer's attempt to explain away the traditional problem of the hermeneutical gap by substituting a linguistic model for the Cartesian psychologistic one should not be taken as a dismissal of historical and cultural differences. In Chapter Four it becomes clear that no thinker is as willing to emphasize such differences as Gadamer. Traditional hermeneutics conceived interpretation as rendering familiar everything that at first appears strange and unfamiliar. Such a theory thus applies a rather authoritarian and dogmatic principle of charity that assumes that the set of true beliefs is everywhere and always largely the same, and that it is also identical to one's own beliefs. Gadamer's philosophical hermeneutics, on the other hand, is structured to preserve the differences and tensions between the text's and the interpreter's horizons of belief, while at the same time affirming the possibility of the interpreter's claim to have understood the text. Unlike Kant who thinks he understands Plato better than Plato understood himself, Gadamer believes we cannot claim to understand Plato's texts better, only differently.

Some philosophers will object that this apparently historicist principle undercuts the very possibility not only of valid interpretation but, more important, of legitimate criticism. Jürgen Habermas, who acknowledges Husserl but not Heidegger as a philosophical parent, criticizes Gadamer for not supplying more explicit grounds for criticism. In their famous debate, recounted in Chapter Four, Habermas contests Gadamer's claim that his hermeneutical philosophy has universal scope because of the involvement of linguisticality in all aspects of human activity. From Habermas's more Marxist perspective, Gadamer's insistence on the universality of language in understanding and knowledge overlooks social determinants of knowledge such as power relations and the work structure. Habermas himself, however, works out a theory of communication that is far more detailed than Gadamer's account of linguisticality, and he too claims universal status for such a theory (calling it "Universal Pragmatics"). He also posits a transcendental and thus apparently unhistorical notion of truth (based on Peirce's consensus theory) that applies in all rational dialogues or discourse situations. Gadamer in turn strongly resists this unhistorical notion of rationality, and insists that there is nothing paradoxical about his own thesis of the historical character of all understanding.

The outcome of these discussions has consequences not only for literary criticism but also for other fields of the humanities. Most of these fields involve an essentially historical dimension. The methodological questions raised in hermeneutics probe into the very possibility of thinking historically. Thus, whether history is viewed as continuous or as discontinuous (involving radical ruptures or paradigm shifts) will make a difference to the kinds of explanations a discipline gives and to the extent to which it searches for causes and general principles. While Gadamer's theory maintains that the interpretive understanding is different, not better, and thus recognizes the possibility of discontinuity between the interpreter and what he interprets, it also makes a central principle of the fact that the interpretation stands in and is conditioned by a tradition. Is it paradoxical to insist both on the possibility of historical discontinuity and on the necessary continuity of the interpreter with his own historical tradition? This must be discussed in detail, especially in the case of the poetic work of art that, as a unique creation, apparently acquires its aesthetic status through its unexpected novelty and its radical transformation of the history of literature. In general, however, it should be clear that by challenging humanist disciplines to think not only about the historical character of their object of study but also about the historical character of their own discipline, Gadamer's philosophical hermeneutics makes a better self-understanding in these disciplines an essential precondition for the legitimacy of their enterprise.

While hermeneutical philosophy offers a theory of understanding and interpretation applicable to all fields of human inquiry, each field has distinctive methodological problems. Applying hermeneutics to jurisprudence or theology, for instance, will require different considerations from those demanded by philology. The field of literary scholarship, however, is a particularly crucial test for a hermeneutical theory. Not only is it clearly concerned with the interpretation of texts but the texts it interprets are the most problematic kind. As works of art, literary and poetic texts appear to stand apart from other, more ordinary uses of language, where the language itself tends to disappear into its use rather than emerge and become visible for its own sake. The resulting philosophical problems about the meaning and value of these aesthetic entities are compounded when the activity of literary criticism enters the picture. The tension is heightened by such contrasts as those between ordinary and poetic language, description and evaluation, and historical influence and aesthetic novelty. Literary criticism finds itself drawn to both poles of these distinctions. It must ask itself whether it is bound to the flow of historical sequence, or whether it can break up time and rearrange the units, either conflating them into an eternal synchrony, as structuralism seems to do, or even inverting the flow through the discovery of backward causations, as Harold Bloom's theory implies.

Gadamer's philosophical hermeneutics intends to revise significantly the fundamental concepts of aesthetics. The practical relevance of these philosophical revisions is most apparent in the new light they project on the basic tenets of interpretive procedures such as formalist literary criticism. Under increasing attack in recent years by literary theorists such as Paul de Man and Geoffrey Hartman, formalism is diagnosed as a method that begins and ends with the observation and analysis of the formal properties of art and thus tends "to isolate the aesthetic fact from its human content."[8] Formalism is thus a catchword that links diverse approaches to literary criticism, ranging from American New Criticism to linguistic structuralism. If I. A. Richards is the original representative of the former, Roland Barthes is exemplary of the latter. Barthes will be considered in the course of this study in order to heighten the contrasts between structuralism and hermeneutics.

Formalism develops as a legitimate reaction to the abuse of historical philology and such methods as biographical and source research, methods that appear irrelevant to the *poetic* aspects of literary texts. Even if this reaction is appropriately motivated, however, it is also an overreaction that tends to eliminate historical dimensions from poetry and its interpretation. Both Hartman and de Man think the task of contemporary criticism is to go beyond formalism, but not in a way that retreats to the historical methods and the theory of language of preformalist philology. A crucial test of the viability of contemporary criticism is whether it can formulate a program of literary history that uses the strengths of formalism and yet avoids its current impasse. The relevance of hermeneutics for recent literary criticism, to be seen in Chapter Five, is that it offers a theoretical formulation of literary history which overcomes the paradoxical tension between the historical nature of interpretation and the aesthetic nature of the poetic text.

Practical criticism itself moves beyond both Cartesian psychology and purely synchronic linguistic theory in the recent development of "reception theory," also to be discussed in Chapter Five. Such a theory explores the consequences of maintaining that literary meaning is not a function of its genetic origin in an author's psyche, nor of purely intrinsic relations between the printed marks on a page, but of its reception in a series of readings (and misreadings) constituting its history of influence. This kind of theory follows philosophical hermeneutics in seeing literary history not as a paradox but as a paradigm for all interpretation. The relative success or failure of this approach is less important than the fact that it represents a development in the history of criticism which parallels the movement in the history of hermeneutics away from psychologism and toward a theory of language that also stresses the temporality and historicity of understanding and interpretation.

Before these connections between practical criticism and philosophical hermeneutics can be discussed in detail, however, the strengths of the alternative positions that insist on formal properties and objective guarantees must be examined and tested. The first chapter, therefore, raises the question of the objectivity of interpretation and investigates the theoretical problems issuing from the representative position of E. D. Hirsch.

ONE

Validity and the Author's Intention: A Critique of E. D. Hirsch's Hermeneutics

Traditional nineteenth-century hermeneutic theory (Schleiermacher, Dilthey) considers understanding to be a process of psychological reconstruction. The object of understanding is the original meaning of a text handed down to the present from a past that is no longer immediately accessible. Reconstruction—which can take place only when there is a bridge between past and present, between text and interpreter—is psychological when this bridge consists of a relation between two persons: the author and the reader. For Dilthey, the text is the "expression" (Ausdruck) of the thoughts and intentions of its author; the interpreter must transpose himself into the author's horizon so as to relive the creative act. The essential link between author and reader, no matter how great the time difference, is a common humanity, a common psychological makeup or generic consciousness, that grounds the intuitive ability to empathize with other persons.[1]

Hermeneutic theory using the notion of psychological reconstruction continues to have force in the twentieth century. A humanistic research that aims at giving a picture of the personalities and minds of great men, a literary interpretation that appeals to the biography of the author, and even a traditional literary history that shows antecedents and sources influencing an author's thinking implicitly tend to presuppose such a theory and its explicit advocates are still in evidence. Most recently E. D. Hirsch,

Jr., has acknowledged his sympathy with Dilthey's notion of empathic *Sichhineinfuhlen* and has reinstated the principle of psychological reconstruction.[2] Hirsch is principally concerned with formulating a theory that makes it possible to speak of the *validity* of interpretations. In the face of what he sees as a dangerous contemporary tendency toward relativism, both in philosophical hermeneutics and in practical criticism, Hirsch considers it necessary to search for criteria to validate interpretations. He feels, however, that such criteria can be applied only under the condition that the basic object of interpretation—that which must be the essential goal of interpretive understanding—is the *author's* intention.

The fact that these criteria all refer ultimately to a psychological construction is hardly surprising when we recall that to verify a text is simply to establish that the author probably meant what we construe his text to mean. The interpreter's primary task is to reproduce in himself the author's "logic," his attitudes, his cultural givens, in short, his world. Even though the process of verification is highly complex and difficult, the ultimate verificative principle is very simple—the imaginative reconstruction of the speaking subject.[3]

Hirsch is aware that the notion of psychological reconstruction generates important philosophical difficulties and that the hermeneutics of Schleiermacher and Dilthey involve major epistemological problems. He wishes to defend some of their insights in terms of more recent advances in linguistics and philosophy of language. His appeal to the language of these earlier hermeneutic theories is intended as criticism of contemporary attitudes that, to his way of thinking, have lost sight of important advantages of these earlier views. The present attitudes that he is contesting are quite variant, ranging from the Anglo-American "New Criticism," which holds that the author's intention is irrelevant to the meaning of a literary text, to Heideggerian hermeneutical philosophy, which maintains that understanding is necessarily rooted in a historical situation.

Hirsch calls the theory common to such unrelated styles of thinking "semantic autonomy." Although Hirsch never precisely defines this theory, it is generally the view that "literature should detach itself from the subjective realm of the author's personal thoughts and feelings" and that "all written language remains independent of that subjective realm" (*VI* 1). Since many present-day literary critics and philosophers find themselves in agreement with such a theory so formulated, it becomes interesting to examine Hirsch's objections to what may be a dominant way of thinking. In opposition to this theory of semantic autonomy, Hirsch makes two major claims about literary meaning: there is "no objectivity [of interpretation] unless meaning itself is unchanging" (*VI* 214); and "meaning is an affair of consciousness not of words" (*VI* 4). These claims need to be explicated and examined more closely to test the viability of Hirsch's attempt to update a hermeneutics oriented toward the reconstruction of the author's intention.

I. MEANING AND SIGNIFICANCE

The attempt to restore the author's intention to a place of preeminence in critics' eyes aims at overcoming skepticism about the possibility of correct interpretation. Given the contemporary proliferation of readings and "approaches," it is understandable that critics are concerned to reaffirm the need for objectivity in interpretation. Faced with the threat of skepticism, however, reaffirmation may go too far in the opposite direction and become dogmatic. There is a difference between objectivity and objectivism. Any interpreter can have a practical interest in seeing that his interpretation will be acceptable to as many readers as possible; objectivity in this practical sense is a matter of degree. Theoretical objectivism, on the other hand, insists that *in principle* there is an unchanging meaning that must be presupposed as the goal of every interpretation if it is to be believed that some interpretations are more true or correct than others. Since new interpretations continue to appear, this objective basis is held out as an indefinite goal, which may never be actualized. In recoiling from skeptical relativism, this theoretical objectivism has to argue that there must be an objective basis without being able to show either that the basis is in fact knowable or that it is ever captured in particular interpretations.

Hirsch risks such dogmatism by claiming that there is "no objectivity unless meaning itself is unchanging" (*VI* 214). This claim is made in reaction to a possible "despair" in view of what

Hirsch, pointing to the current proliferation of so many new interpretations and new methods of interpreting, calls the "babel of interpretations" (*VI* 129). His major project is to show that at least in principle such a babel is not necessarily a feature of literary interpretation. At the same time he is specifically fighting a skepticism about objectivity that he sees in what he considers "radical historicism" in Heidegger and Gadamer. Hirsch makes the counterclaim that while the *importance* of a work may vary with time and within different interpretive contexts, the one underlying meaning of the work does not change. The meaning of the text—which, on this account, is the author's willed meaning—is said to be self-identical, determinate, and reproducible (that is, shareable rather than private). The understanding that grasps this determinate and unchanging meaning is totally neutral and unsullied by the interpreter's own normative goals or his views of the work's importance. Only on such grounds, Hirsch believes, is it possible to speak of the validity of interpretation.

To understand Hirsch's claims it is necessary to understand his terminology. For Hirsch, and for traditional hermeneutics, the distinction between the *subtilitas intelligendi* and the *subtilitas explicandi* (*VI* 129) is crucial. The former notion refers to the construction of the text's meaning in its own terms, while the latter refers to the explanation of the meaning, perhaps in terms different from those of the text but more familiar to the interpreter and his audience. While the word "interpretation" normally refers to both moments, Hirsch uses the word "understanding" for the *subtilitas intelligendi* and the word "interpretation" for the *subtilitas explicandi* (*VI* 136).

"Understanding" and "interpretation" must be further distinguished from other moments of the interpretive process—"judgment" and "criticism." While understanding and interpretation differ in that the former involves the construction of meaning and the latter its explanation, both have as their object the meaning of the text per se. On Hirsch's account a text has not only "meaning" but also "significance." (Hirsch uses the German word *Sinn* for the former and *Bedeutung* for the latter.) Verbal meaning is what the author meant to say, and the construction of that meaning by the interpreter is called *understanding*. The explanation of that understanding is *interpretation*. Interpretation often shades off into evaluation, however, judging the text in terms of external considerations. This act of *judgment,* construing a relation between the text and something else, can then itself be explained and discussed, and this latter activity is what Hirsch calls *criticism.* While the object of understanding and interpretation is "meaning," the object of judgment and criticism is "significance"—that is, any perceived relationship between the verbal meaning of the text and something else (*VI* 143).

What follows for the relation of understanding and interpretation to meaning also follows for the relation of judgment and criticism to significance. Given these distinctions Hirsch can claim that even varying *interpretations* need not conflict with one another, for they can be said to presuppose a common *understanding* of the text. While the explanation of this understanding may cause interpreters to express themselves differently, basically they must be talking about the same thing: the understanding of the text in its own terms. There can be only one correct understanding, therefore; otherwise the text has not, in fact, been understood in its own terms but in some other way. Similarly, ways of expressing criticism can vary while the basic judgment of the significance of the work can remain the same (*VI* 144).

Confusing understanding and interpretation, the *subtilitas intelligendi* and the *subtilitas explicandi,* is, for Hirsch, a capital mistake. The consequent skepticism about the possibility of attaining a valid (perspective-free or value-free) understanding of a text is found by Hirsch principally in the hermeneutical philosophies of Heidegger and Gadamer. The difficulty with Hirsch's account, however, is that while he thinks the distinction is almost intuitively obvious and necessary, others will find it much less self-evident. Hirsch himself mentions that in most practical commentary on literary texts, all four functions (understanding, interpretation, judgment, and criticism) are present and that they will be difficult to distinguish from one another (*VI* 130, 140). He even notes that understanding is "silent," while interpretation is "garrulous" (*VI* 135). Thus understanding is not what actually gets written down in the act of practical commentary. Rather, only interpretation appears; the commentary is always in the interpreter's terms and not in the text's.

Given the blending of these two moments in actual commentary, however, the arguments for the primacy of "silent" understanding over interpretive explanation of the text will be based on appeal to logical necessity and not to actual practice. Thus Hirsch argues that his notion of an objective understanding is necessary because he thinks there must be one common structure to which the various interpretations refer:

> To understand an utterance it is, in fact, not just desirable but absolutely unavoidable that we understand it in its own terms. We could not possibly recast a text's meanings in different terms unless we had already understood the text in its own.   [*VI* 134]

This statement might surprise some readers who suppose that a text is first understood in different terms before it is discovered whether these terms are *too* different: college freshmen and university professors alike interpret the text in terms different from the text's, but more often than not the interpretations of the latter are more likely to be appropriate than those of the students. The notion of ever understanding a text "in its own terms" might seem only an ideal, even an unattainable one.

Such a reaction is likely to be greeted by Hirsch as a sign of the skepticism he deplores. In fact, similar intuitions lie behind the views of Gadamer and Heidegger, and Hirsch counters this "skeptical historicism" with the following rebuttal:

> The skeptical historicist infers too much from the fact that present-day experiences, categories, and modes of thought are not the same as those of the past. He concludes that we can only understand a text in *our* own terms, but this is a contradictory statement since verbal meaning has to be construed in *its* own terms if it is to be construed at all.   [*VI* 135]

And further:

> The skeptical historicist...converts the plausible idea that the mastery of unfamiliar meanings is arduous and uncertain into the idea that we always have to impose our own alien conventions and associations. But this is simply not true. If we do not construe a text in what we rightly or wrongly assume to be its own terms then we do not construe it at all. We do not understand anything that we could subsequently recast in our own terms.   [*VI* 135]

As these passages suggest, the question is not how "understanding" and "interpretation" can be distinguished in actual practice.

Rather, the distinction serves a more a priori function. The real argument between Hirsch and his imagined "skepticist" opponent is not so much a practical as a philosophical one: must the interpreter believe that there is one right understanding of the text or may he believe that there is no one right understanding but only more or less appropriate interpretations? In line with this perhaps "skeptical" alternative it may also be believed that there is no such thing as *the* meaning of a text (even in Hirsch's strict sense as distinct from significance)—which is to say, in Hirsch's language, that textual meaning is not strictly "determinate."

An important part of the burden of Hirsch's theory rests on his arguments that meaning is in fact determinate and unchanging. Unfortunately, these conclusions follow from his special terminology rather than from generally observable experiences. Hirsch thinks it necessary to posit two qualities of meaning if interpretation is to be possible: reproducibility, which is to say that meaning is shareable; and determinacy. This latter term does not mean definiteness or preciseness, since Hirsch claims that meaning can be determinate but ambiguous (see *VI* 44-45). Rather he intends it merely to convey that a meaning is always identical with itself.

These qualities need to be established not just by definition but by argument, however, if Hirsch is to argue successfully that textual meaning is the unchanging basis for valid interpretation. Yet at the beginning of his discussion of verbal meaning it appears that reproducibility will be proved when determinacy is proved, and he gives a promise for the proof of determinacy.

The reproducibility (and thus the sharability) of verbal meaning depends on there being something to reproduce. For the moment I will assume that any verbal meaning as defined above is a determinate entity with a boundary that discriminates what is from what is not. [*VI* 31-32]

Yet when the discussion of determinacy begins after the discussion of reproducibility, it turns out that determinacy is only proved insofar as it is shown to follow from the definition of reproducibility.

Reproducibility is a quality of verbal meaning that makes interpretation possible: if meaning were not reproducible, it could not be actualized by someone else and therefore could not be understood or interpreted. Determinacy, on the other hand, is a quality of meaning required in order that there *be* something to reproduce. Determinacy is a necessary attribute of any sharable meaning, since an indeterminacy cannot be shared: if a meaning were indeterminate, it would have no boundaries, no self-identity, and therefore could have no identity with a meaning entertained by someone else.   [*VI* 44]

Hirsch's only further arguments are negative, directed against various formulations of relativistic positions holding that the meaning of texts can change. His present statement only begs the question of whether meaning is unchanging. He begins by noting that there cannot be reproducibility without determinate meaning and goes on to assert that since there is reproducibility, it follows that there must be determinate meaning.

The argument commits what can be called, following Hirsch's own cue, the Cinderella fallacy. This fallacy grows out of the dogmatic belief that if we think a thing must be there, then it is in fact there, even if it can never be seen. This blend of begging the question and hasty ontologizing surfaces in the following passage.

If a meaning can change its identity and in fact does, then we have no norm for judging whether we are encountering the real meaning in a changed form or some spurious meaning that is pretending to be the one we seek. Once it is admitted that a meaning can change its characteristics, then there is no way of finding the true Cinderella among all the contenders. There is no dependable glass slipper we can use as a test, since the old slipper will no longer fit the new Cinderella. To the interpreter this lack of a stable normative principle is equivalent to the indeterminacy of meaning.   [*VI* 46]

The whole point of insisting on the distinction between understanding and interpretation seemed to be to establish that there was some understanding which fit the literary text such that it was the meaning of the text and not just of the critic's reaction to the text. In other words, the point was to establish that there was a glass slipper that guarantees the validity of the real Cinderella. Accordingly, Hirsch thinks that it tells against "skeptical relativists" that they would not be able to believe that their interpretive slipper could ever be said to fit the true Cinderella. Yet Hirsch's account does not seem to do a better job in explaining the possibility of the shoe fitting the foot. What guides the explication is the interpreter's "understanding" of the text and, for Hirsch, of the author's intention. To find Cinderella—that is, the version that is really the literary text—we need only find out whom the shoe fits. This seems fine until we ask how we know that we have discovered the author's intention. To this the answer will be, try it on Cinderella. But now we are right back where we started, since the original problem is that we do not know who Cinderella is. Unfortunately the proof for the possibility of objective, valid commentary in Hirsch's theory hinges on the notion of determinacy of meaning, and the proof of the latter depends on the former.

This circularity makes it necessary to look more closely at Hirsch's terms. How does he construe "verbal meaning," and what would "determinacy" look like in interpretive practice? There is a close connection between Hirsch's thesis that meaning is objective and unchanging and his other thesis that "meaning is an affair of consciousness and not of words." In focusing on this point, Hirsch's central concern is to combat the theory of "semantic autonomy" in order to reinstate the author's intention as the principal interpretive criterion. In their understanding of a text, interpreters are said to be "completely subservient to [the author's] will, because the meaning of his utterance is the meaning he wills to convey" (*VI* 142). Hirsch clearly presupposes a theory of meaning that connects meaning with the will of a psychological agent. This position puts him at odds with currently important epistemological and literary-critical theories that challenge such a close connection between intention and meaning. The concept of meaning itself needs careful analysis.

When Hirsch claims that "meaning is an affair of consciousness not of words" (*VI* 4), he is implicitly presenting a theory of meaning.[4] He defines *"verbal meaning"* as "whatever someone has willed to convey by a particular sequence of linguistic signs and which can be conveyed (shared) by means of those linguistic signs" (*VI* 31). The difficulty with the theory is that leaving the term "whatever" unclarified in terms of important philosophical issues leads to open-ended argumentation. Because the "whatever" is contrasted with the linguistic signs or "words," it is apparently to be taken as something distinct from the words themselves, and even as linguistically independent or neutral, since for Hirsch the meaning of the verbal utterance is determined by inferring the speaker's intentions (see *VI* 4). But this inference clearly begs Hirsch's question about meaning. Though it may explain how we come to decide between different possible meanings of the utterance, it does not make it clear how that utterance can have those different possible meanings to start with, and does not establish consciousness as the determinant of meaning.

Hirsch goes on to note that a verbal meaning is a *"willed type"* (*VI* 51)—that is, a "whole meaning" that is willed (intended) and which thus may include particular conscious or subconscious submeanings (*VI* 49). A *type,* an appendix concludes, is a "mental object" or an "idea" (*VI* 265). Furthermore, the idea expressed by an utterance is the "intrinsic genre" of the utterance. "Intrinsic genre," a key term in Hirsch's theory, is that meaning which stays the same despite the possibility of variation in the arrangement or selection of particular words in the utterance. Hirsch never convincingly argues that changing a word does not change the sense, being content with an example he considers self-evident: substituting "happy" for "blissful" in a passage from Milton (*VI* 84-85). This example, however, is not persuasive, since "happy" connotes contentment, whereas "blissful" suggests ecstasy or exaltation, and thus the preceding phrases might also be cast in a different light. The example only shows that the thoughts expressed are definitely not precisely the same. Similarity is not equivalence.[5]

Attempts to pin down the notion of intrinsic genre result in an unfortunate circle. Genre is said to be the *purpose* of a person, what he wills or intends (*VI* 99-101). In this case, however, the purpose is to communicate an idea. But "idea," we are told, is not to be construed too generally or abstractly, as it is unique to the utterance and is thus what the intrinsic genre of the utterance is. The circularity of this explanation, resulting from its emptiness, tends to give rise to the suspicion that Hirsch has fallen victim to what Quine calls the "idea idea."[6] He has failed to see that our knowledge of ideas is not independent of our language; rather, it depends on our possession of language, especially one with such terms as "idea" and "concept."

To clarify, consider the situation of a person's claim, when he reflects or is challenged on a statement, that he did not mean what he said. Hirsch (*VI* 78-88) argues that in this case the intended or willed meaning is a whole (a "type" idea or intrinsic genre) not actually instantiated in the words of the statement. Subsequent revision of the wording is in accordance with the intended genre.

But it is precisely this case that normally causes the need to distinguish between meaning and intending, for it leads to the assumption that what a person means to say ("intends") does not *necessarily* make a difference to the meaning of what is said. The words do not take their meaning from the intentions but have an autonomous meaning; otherwise there would be no conflict. Hirsch does not explain "meaning" as such but distinguishes among different kinds of meaning. For him it is a question of generic meanings, or ideas, as distinct from particular meanings—that is, particular arrangements of words. This is at variance with his appeal to the author's intention in order to *explain* meaning as a function "of consciousness not of words."

The "explanation" is circular, and at best empty: it comes down to saying "we use words as we do because we have the concepts we have"[7]—a sentence that seems to explain but in fact only repeats the claim. Hirsch himself admits that, although he believes that we must distinguish between the intrinsic genre (generic meaning) and the particular meaning of particular utterances, it is not possible to look at a particular utterance and say " '*This* is the intrinsic genre of the meaning, and *that* is the meaning in its particularity' " (*VI* 82). But the explanation that the words' meanings are ideas is empty if it turns out that the ideas are merely those same words.

Another crucial obscurity in Hirsch's notion of meaning stems from the fact that he overlooks the difference between talking about meaning from the point of view of sentences and discussing it from the point of view of texts. He never justifies his inference that examples and arguments at the level of sentences also apply at the level of texts, and vice versa. Yet "meaning" can mean different things in these two cases. A sentence can have several meanings, and I may choose one and not another because I know the "meaning" of the text or the context as a whole; that is to say, I think I understand the context or purpose that provides clues as to how I am intended to take the particular sentence. Furthermore, even on Hirsch's own terms the meaning of a text is a construct and thus takes place over an observable stretch of time, during which sentences are being understood instantaneously. This lack of analogy between the two kinds of understanding makes at least a prima facie case that one cannot infer from the one sort of case to the other without further explanation. Equating the two cases can also lead to illicit arguments and to fundamental confusions, as seems to occur at the very beginning of Hirsch's attempt to formulate his most important distinction, that between the meaning of a text (which does not change) and its significance (the use to which the text is put and which varies). Hirsch claims that his distinction between the meaning of a text and its significance was also made by Frege in the paper "Über Sinn und Bedeutung" (see *VI* 211). But the "text" Hirsch discusses is merely one sentence—such as "Scott is the author of *Waverly*" or "The Evening Star is the Morning Star," where two different meanings are expressed (the "Evening Star" and the "Morning Star"), with only one referent or *Bedeutung* (the planet Venus). But since texts, or collections of sentences, often take their meaning precisely from the interrelations among the various sentences, Hirsch would have to elaborate his argument to get from a sentence to a text. Frege's own arguments count against Hirsch's enterprise. There is little evidence that Frege's distinction between *Sinn* and *Bedeutung* (better translated as "sense" and "reference") has any relation to Hirsch's meaning-significance distinction. Whereas Hirsch holds that meaning (= *Sinn;* see *VI* 216) is permanent while *Bedeutung* or significance may change, Frege in this essay sees *Bedeutung* (or the reference of a sentence) as related to a truth-value (eventually either "the True" or "the False"). It is also well known that for Frege thoughts (or *Gedanken*—that is, the *Sinn* of a sentence), *if true,* are true eternally (or atemporally). Thus it is not the case, in Frege's terms, that the reference or truth-value of a thought changes; change occurs only in the belief that the thought is true or not true.[8]

Frege would, in fact, be entirely opposed to Hirsch's central theses. One of these is the rejection of the distinction in principle between poetic texts and ordinary, nonpoetic texts (see *VI* 1, 210, 248). The collapse of this distinction is, for Hirsch, a corollary of his supposedly Fregean meaning-significance distinction, "meaning" being what the author has willed. Yet Frege clearly holds that there is an essential difference between poetic and nonpoetic (or, specifically, scientific) language. He also holds what Hirsch calls the theory of semantic autonomy, for the meanings of sentences (if true) are, on Frege's account, independent of their "thinker." Frege's *Sinn-Bedeutung* distinction cannot be used by Hirsch, for

Frege defines *Bedeutung* in such a way that poetic language has no *Bedeutung* but only *Sinn*.[9] On this view poetic language is neither true nor false, for there is no referent for the word *moly* (a magical plant described by Homer) and probably none for "Odysseus" (although the words do, of course, have a sense).[10] Furthermore, a thought—the name given by Frege to the sense (Sinn) of a sentence —unlike a mental image (Vorstellung), is not, when it is true, a special property of a thinker but is accessible in the same way to all who desire to understand it (and who speak the language). The meaning is, as it were, "written on the wall" for all to see, and Frege affirms that "it is completely indifferent for the understanding to know *who* wrote it down."[11] To support this position, Frege argues that if meanings (true or false thoughts) were less "impersonal," two people could not be said to think the same thought, and the truth of a statement (such as $2 + 2 = 4$) could not be debated (since it would mean something different to each party in the debate). Frege thus has no sympathy for Hirsch's central thesis that meaning is determined by authorial will.

Although Hirsch claims that his meaning-significance distinction is grounded in Frege, the positions he hopes to refute by the use of that distinction turn out to be ones for which Frege is famous and which he held more radically than many other philosophers. The irony casts doubt not only on the clarity of Hirsch's fundamental distinction but also on his ultimate success in avoiding the trap of psychologism that Frege had clearly warned against. Hirsch's insistence on meaning as an affair of the consciousness of actual persons is either psychologistic or merely redundant, since it does not say anything about meaning beyond linking it to sentences. The further "explanation" achieved by linking sentences to consciousness is either extraneous or explains something else, such as speech acts or practical activity.

Certainly the difficulties in clarifying Hirsch's notion of meaning do not demonstrate that his theory of interpretation is invalid. Unless important steps in the theory can be filled in, however, the account remains incomplete and inadequate. The theory leaps from the claim that the "author's or speaker's subjective act is formally necessary to verbal meaning" to the conclusion that the author or speaker is the "specifier of meaning" (see, for example, *VI* 225-226). Such a leap omits much that would have to be justified. Furthermore, very little follows from the premise that the author's act is "formally necessary" to meaning. Such a claim can at best be trivially true, for it merely says something to the effect that instances of language are produced by creatures capable of language. The task of generating a theory of meaning or even of communication is not helped thereby.

Hirsch draws the distinctions between meaning and significance and between understanding and interpretation to avoid a circular theory of interpretation. The hope is that a more "linear" theory of textual commentary—one positing a necessary understanding as a formal basis from which interpretive conclusions then follow —will produce an objective foundation for the possibility of valid interpretation. Hirsch argues that it is necessary at least to posit one correct understanding of the text in order to assert that particular interpretations are more or less in accord with it and therefore are or are not valid, given the current evidence. It must be concluded, however, that Hirsch's objectivist intuitions have led him too far toward dogmatism. A sufficient answer to skeptical relativism argues that some interpretations are at least *falsifiable.* The claim of falsifiability does not entail the belief that *verifiability* is necessarily attainable. To posit an unchanging meaning as the basis for an adequate understanding is to add a further step. Even the mention of *validating* interpretations—although it is a weaker claim because it recognizes the incompleteness of evidence—presupposes, at least in Hirsch's theory, this "unchanging" meaning that can only be dogmatically asserted and never captured. Falsifiability as a condition of interpretation provides objectivity at least to some degree and thus suffices to overcome skeptical relativism. To combat relativism with a theoretical objectivism that insists on the principle of unchanging meaning and one proper understanding is philosophical overkill.

The question remains as to whether, despite the difficulties in its *theoretical* formulation, Hirsch's position has *practical* advantages. If so, the theoretical problems definitely merit further thought. The theory is, in fact, intended to have the practical consequence of changing some current beliefs about what constitutes evidence. Hirsch's insistence on the author's intention as the determinant of textual meaning has been widely received as a new basis for rejecting the formalist practice of Anglo-American New Criticism.

II. THE AUTHOR'S INTENTION

In everyday discourse, where words serve other purposes than they often do in clear and distinct reasoning, the speaker's meaning is determined not only by the content of his utterances but also by his intention to perform some act. The poet's or author's intention thus appears to be natural ground for explicating the meaning of the literary text. The philosophical difficulties begin when it becomes a question of clarifying the notions of "meaning" and "intention" in the latter case. Literary language is much less ordinary than everyday discourse, and its analysis raises a number of additional questions tied to philosophical aesthetics. Philosophical *hermeneutics* has always been the enterprise that concerns itself with those problems that overlap both aesthetics and epistemology in dealing with the nature of literary language and communication. Hence a review of the debate in literary criticism provides relevant background for more general hermeneutical problems.

The essay that is perhaps the fundamental manifesto of Anglo-American New Criticism is "The Intentional Fallacy,"[12] representing the collaboration of a literary critic, William Wimsatt, Jr., and a philosopher, Monroe Beardsley. Implicitly criticizing a pre-Wittgensteinian notion of intention, these writers argue that a major fallacy underlies the inference that uses authorial intention as a criterion for establishing the meaning of a literary text. More recently Hirsch has attempted to defend a new intentionalism as a basis for his notion of validity in interpretation. His attempt at a philosophical clarification of the notion of intention appeals to the famous phenomenological notion of intentionality developed by Edmund Husserl. The initial impression of Hirsch's new intentionalism is that it will affect practical interpretation by justifying anew the appeal to the author's own attitudes and beliefs about his work. The dispute about the critic's access to the authorial intention is purportedly not trivial, and Wimsatt and Beardsley in fact state that "There is hardly a problem of literary criticism in which the critic's approach will not be qualified by his view of 'intention'" (*Verbal Icon* 3). It remains to be seen whether Hirsch's new intentionalism makes a significant difference in critics' estimation of the evidence needed as proof of the meaning of literary texts.

"Intention," Wimsatt and Beardsley write in "The Intentional Fallacy," "is design or plan in the author's mind." It therefore has "obvious affinities for the author's attitude toward his work, the way he felt, what made him write" (*Verbal Icon* 4). Intention is thus conceived of as mental and basically private. The essay distinguishes between the notion of intention in the designing intellect as a *cause* of the literary work and the notion of intention as a *standard*. The *fallacy* for these anti-intentionalists occurs only when intention is taken as a standard, and the authors hold that intention is "neither available nor desirable as a standard for judging the success of a work of literary art" (*Verbal Icon* 3).[13] Intention as standard is the point on which the intentionalist, Hirsch, ostensibly attacks the anti-intentionalists, Wimsatt and Beardsley.

Although New Criticism is often thought to exclude biographical evidence about the author's intention entirely, such a conclusion is not entailed by "The Intentional Fallacy." Wimsatt and Beardsley clearly state, "The use of biographical evidence need not involve intentionalism, because while it may be evidence of what the author intended, it may also be evidence of the meaning of his words and the dramatic character of his utterance" (*Verbal Icon* 11). Because the use of biographical evidence often permits the intentional inference, however, evidence intrinsic to the text is preferred. The fallacy occurs only when the critic confuses the intention with the standard for determining what the actual meaning of the literary text is.

> One must ask how a critic expects to get an answer to the question about intention. How is he to find out what the poet tried to do? If the poet succeeded in doing it, then the poem itself shows what he was trying to do. And if the poet did not succeed, then the poem is not adequate evidence, and the critic must go outside the poem—for evidence of an intention that did not become effective in the poem.   [*Verbal Icon* 4]

The question of intention, then, centers on the genesis of the poem, the process of its coming into being. The critic's question is somewhat different, concerning not the genesis but the actual achievement—the result of the process, not the process itself. The "intentional fallacy" is thus a version of the "genetic fallacy," which involves confusing process and result.

Genetic considerations are not always irrelevant, however, and it is not always a fallacy to discuss achievement and process simultaneously. In everyday discourse, for instance, knowing the background or context of an utterance can be relevant to an understanding of what the utterance (as speech act) in fact means. Even if the utterance is so elliptical as to make no sense in and of itself, the intention of the speaker may be correctly inferred. This is not, however, a counterargument against the anti-intentionalists. Wimsatt and Beardsley certainly allow for the notion of intention in practical speech: "poetry differs from practical messages, which are successful if and only if we correctly infer the intention" (*Verbal Icon* 5). In practical speech the language is simply a means to an end, a tool to convey a meaning. In such a case the meaning is intimately linked with the agent's intention. Poetic language as an art, on the other hand, is an end in itself, and if it is possible to distinguish between the author and his works, if the author's meaning is something other than what he has created, then he has failed. In that sense a good intentionalist interpretation, one truly showing the intention of the author as separable from the work, implies that the poem is bad. Such a poem would not be a complete whole, an end in itself, but could only be understood through additional information about the creative intention.

These arguments will not dissuade the adamant intentionalist. Quite legitimately, for instance, he can refuse to recognize such a sharp difference between poetry and ordinary language, between art and life. This is precisely what Hirsch does, although without the necessary argumentation. Furthermore, Hirsch goes on to use the arguments of the anti-intentionalists to argue that the intention *must* be the object of critical investigation. Thus the intentionalist Hirsch agrees with the anti-intentionalists Wimsatt and Beardsley that the private intentions of the author's mind are not accessible and that public meanings alone are available. Whereas the anti-intentionalists use this point to rule out intention, the intentionalist infers from it that the intention is precisely what the critic is seeking after all. Hirsch writes:

Whenever an interpretation manages to convince another person, that in itself proves beyond doubt that the author's words *can* publicly imply such a meaning. Since the interpreted meaning *was* conveyed to another person, indeed to at least two other persons, the only significant interpretive question is, "Did the author really intend that public meaning by his words?" [*VI* 15]

The intentionalist thus suggests that only the author's intention will provide the basis for properly adjudicating between conflicting construals of the text.

Hirsch also inverts another point that Wimsatt and Beardsley take to be axiomatic—that the intention cannot possibly function as a *standard* but can only be conceived as a cause in the author's mind and that it is therefore relevant only to a theory of poetic genesis and not to a theory of interpretation. Hirsch argues that one sense of "standard" makes intention irrelevant to the meaning of the text—that is, when it becomes a question of evaluating the *effectiveness* of the actual way in which the intention was expressed. He thinks that it is fallacious to appeal to intention as a standard only in judging a poem. But this is a trivial point; if it were true, no poem would be judged negatively, since most poets have positive intentions insofar as they at least intend their poems to be successful. Certainly the sense of the word "standard" as used by the anti-intentionalists is not exhausted by Hirsch's point. Thus when Hirsch goes on to hold that the intention is necessary for determining what the poem is saying (whether successfully or unsuccessfully), he *is* antithetically opposed, not only to the popular understanding of "The Intentional Fallacy" but also to the anti-intentionalists themselves. His claim that he is to be considered "in essential agreement with the American anti-intentionalists" (*VI* 243) is therefore questionable. In fact, he uses the case of the unsuccessful poem for purposes opposite those of the anti-intentionalists. They use this case to show that intention is not at play in critical judgment, arguing that the intention is not to be found in the poem, for even if the poet failed, one would have to go outside the poem to find the intention. Precisely this move of finding a discrepancy between intention and accomplishment, however, is what demonstrates to the intentionalist the need to retain the intention as the proper object of determining what it is that the poem is saying. Thus, supposing a poem intended to convey a sense of desolation but actually leaves readers only with an impression that the sea is wet or that dusk is falling, Hirsch argues,

the intentional fallacy has no proper application whatever to verbal meaning. In the above example the only universally valid meaning of the poem is the sense of desolation. If the critic has not understood that point, he will not even reach an accurate judgment—namely, that the meaning was ineptly expressed and perhaps was not worth expressing in the first place.   [*VI* 12]

Whereas the anti-intentionalists see intention as extrinsic, the intentionalist sees it as intrinsic and asks only whether it is adequately actualized or not.

When the arguments against intentionalism reappear as arguments for intentionalism, we suspect that a different notion of intention is now involved. In fact, although Hirsch speaks of the author's intention as if it were the "old-fashioned ideal" (*VI* 26) that is normally understood, and hence the same concept against which the anti-intentionalists argue, he has actually changed the notion of intention considerably. For Hirsch intention is a linguistic term, the verbal meaning that is essentially shareable, rather than a psychological term, a private meaning in the author's mind. His notion of intention is closer to what phenomenologists mean by the term "intentionality"—a process of consciousness according to which "*different* intentional acts (on different occasions) 'intend' an *identical* intentional object" (*VI* 218). Roughly the analogy is with acts of perception; hence, though a perceiver can only see an object—for example, a tree—from a particular perspective, and though different perceivers see different aspects of that object, there remains only one perceptual object. Moreover, the object is the same in different acts of perception, whether at different times or at the same time by different perceivers.

Hirsch hopes to avoid psychologism on the one hand and the relativism of radical historicism on the other by appealing to the phenomenological analysis of intentionality and showing that the text has one meaning that stays the same despite the passage of time or different methods of interpretive perception. There are several respects in which his appeal to this notion of intentionality is philosophically unclear. Hirsch mentions in a footnote to an appendix (*VI* 218) that the term "intention" as used by literary critics to mean a purpose of an author is distinct from the sense in which it is used by phenomenologists as a description of the activity of consciousness; he himself, however, does not make clear in subsequent occurrences of the term which sense he is using. From the philosophical notion per se there is little that would follow for the purposes of the practical literary critic, for as Hirsch himself remarks, "in the literary usage, which involves problems of rhetoric, it is possible to speak of an unfulfilled intention, while in Husserl's usage such a locution would be meaningless" (*VI* 218). What is discussed in phenomenology is the activity of any act of consciousness, not the question of the standards by which to evaluate particular judgments. In fact, a related problem that accompanies Husserl's account concerns the difficulty he has explaining our assurance that we are seeing a real tree and not just hallucinating one. Husserl's intentional object is still a mental object, not strictly identified with a real thing, for the description occurs when the "natural attitude" (in which the existence of real things in the world is presupposed) has been suspended.

In another and more general respect, the analogy with the Husserlian account of perception can be misleading, for the analogy does not go very far. A perception of a tree is an immediate act of consciousness, whereas understanding the meaning of a text is a reflective, mediated procedure. Hirsch explicitly states that "There is no immediacy in understanding" and often insists that the understanding involved in the *subtilitas intelligendi* is a *"construction"* (see, for example, *VI* 43, 136). What is true, however, of an activity where an object is immediately present is not necessarily true of an activity where there is no immediately given object.

Furthermore, much of the argument about verbal meaning as an intentional object becomes opaque when the distinction between the "meaning" of individual sentences and the "meaning" of texts is overlooked. The claim is made that the interpreter cannot narrow down possible meanings to probable meanings unless he posits a speaker who means something definite (*VI* 225). Yet once again the argument for this claim is given on the basis of a single sentence that is then shown in isolation to have a wide possible range of interpretations. Hirsch's example is not convincing when a text, and not just an isolated sentence, is at stake, since by their interaction the written sentences in a text themselves narrow down the range of possible interpretations.

There are serious doubts, then, that Hirsch's attempt to connect intention and intentionality retains the features of the notion of intention most at issue in the debate about the viability of intentionalist criticism. Furthermore, since Hirsch is changing the meaning of the concepts involved, he is not really rebutting the anti-intentionalists. Literary critics will want to know whether Hirsch's new intentionalism at least allows a different kind of evidence or emphasis in determining the meaning of texts than does

the anti-intentionalism of Wimsatt and Beardsley, or of New Criticism in general.

The first confirmation of the suspicion that the evidence will not
be substantially different is found when we ask about the identity
of the "author" in Hirsch's theory of the author's intention.
When he asserts that the appeal to the author's intention is the sole
basis for validity in interpretation, is the "author" here the same
biographical person rejected as irrelevant by the anti-intentionalists?

In point of fact, in an appendix Hirsch implies that the author
being interpreted is not the "biographical person" but a *linguistic*
construct—the "speaking subject."

> The speaking subject is not, however, identical with the subjectivity of the author
> as an actual historical person.... The speaking subject may be defined as the
> final and most comprehensive level of awareness determinative of verbal mean-
> ing. In the case of a lie, the speaking subject assumes that he tells the truth, while
> the actual subject retains a private awareness of his deception. Similarly, many
> speakers retain in their isolated privacy a self-conscious awareness of their verbal
> meaning, an awareness which may agree or disagree, approve or disapprove, but
> which does not participate in determining their verbal meaning. To interpreta-
> tion, this level of awareness is as irrelevant as it is inaccessible. In construing and
> verifying verbal meaning, only the speaking subject counts.   [*VI* 242, 244]

As the case of the lie indicates, the speaking subject is clearly determined only from the meaning of the words themselves. Hirsch's
new intentionalism therefore seems identical with the old anti-
intentionalism, except for a different and much more complicated
vocabulary. His speaking subject looks, after all, very much like
what Wimsatt and Beardsley called the "dramatic speaker" and
which is also a function of the text itself. One of their main points
was that "We ought to impute the thoughts and attitudes of the
poem immediately to the dramatic *speaker,* and if to the author at
all, only by an act of biographical inference" (*Verbal Icon* 5).

Hirsch is, of course, correct in noting that knowledge about the
biographical author and his historical setting will influence the
reader in the process of coming to an understanding of the text.
Anti-intentionalism can also accept this circumstance without any
difficulty. But the validity of an understanding is not necessarily
determined by its genesis. If Hirsch does not agree with this point,

he himself has undercut the possibility of validity in interpretation.

At this point it becomes clear that Hirsch's theory is to be discussed at the theoretical, philosophical level, and not at the level of the actual practice of literary interpretation. The discussion of the author's intention normally occurs at the level of a discussion about the appropriateness of certain kinds of evidence. At the level of philosophical hermeneutics, however, while the question of different kinds of evidence is important, the general concern is more with *beliefs about* the nature of interpretation than with various techniques of actual interpretation.

That Hirsch's theory does not have real force as a theory of evidence can be seen in the fact that his appeal to the author's intention cannot be "cashed in." When the question becomes one concerning criteria for deciding between different, and even conflicting, interpretations, it turns out that the interpreter does not have a piece of evidence—the author's intention in the usual sense—that he can turn to as a guarantee for certainty. It seems instead that the interpreter has captured the author's intended meaning only if his interpretation is valid.

This point becomes clear in the last chapter of *Validity in Interpretation,* where Hirsch argues that interpretations are only probable at best and their validity contingent upon the evidence at hand. Since evidence is never complete, Hirsch allows, absolute certainty can never be attained. The question is not whether particular interpretations are correct but whether it is essential to believe in one right understanding in order to claim correctness for a particular interpretation. This is the question Hirsch is really addressing; he believes in addition that the correct understanding will necessarily be identical with the author's intended meaning.

As soon as anyone claims validity for his interpretation (and few would listen to a critic who did not), he is immediately caught in a web of logical necessity. If his claim to validity is to hold, he must be willing to measure his interpretation against a genuinely discriminating norm, and the only compelling normative principle that has ever been brought forward is the old-fashioned ideal of rightly understanding what the author meant.   [*VI* 26]

Yet there is reason to doubt that the notion of intention as Hirsch has defined it is a "genuinely discriminating norm" that can be used to distinguish between interpretations. Hirsch's claim that there is no way of "defining in principle the nature of correct interpretation" *without* the author's intention (*VI* 226) does allow the textual interpretation to absorb such data as information about the typical attitudes and usages of the author; but it is not clear that such external aids are excluded by anti-intentionalism. More important, the data have limitations in themselves, for the "typical" attitudes do not exclude the possibility that an untypical or atypical occurrence obtains in a given case.

Basically, then, Hirsch's idea that the author's intention is the only basis for defining correct interpretation is a philosophical rather than a practical point. Furthermore, its philosophical force appears to be more that of a regulative principle in a Kantian sense. That is to say, since the author's meaning is to be *constructed* in the process of understanding, but since certainty is never attainable, the goal is held out as an ideal one. Such a notion gives an interpreter grounds on which to assert that his interpretation is correct—insofar as he *believes* that it approaches the right understanding and that there is a "right" understanding to be approached. But regulative principles run the danger of being empty. Often no account is given of how the particular empirical situation does or does not measure up to the ideal specified in the principle. If the notion of the author's intended meaning is only regulative, the interpreter has nothing against which to criticize his own understanding. He has no recourse beyond the dogmatic assertion that his understanding is true. Such an empty principle is dangerous because it can undercut the awareness of the limitations of the interpretation and lead to a forgetting of the need for self-criticism.

In this regard the question of kinds of evidence differs from the philosophical question of the *form* of correct procedure in interpretation. An interpretation, though it is correct, can be rejected as invalid if its arguments are fallacious or if it is correct for the wrong reasons. Conceptually "validity" and "verification" can be separated even more sharply than Hirsch does when he relinquishes the latter term in favor of the former. Validity means that, once all the relevant evidence is taken into account, the interpretation is internally consistent. Of two different interpretations based on the same "reading" of the text, one may be invalid and the other valid. That an interpretation is valid in this sense, however, does not necessarily mean that it is true, at least in more than a trivial sense. An "interpretation" such as "All the phrases of 'Les Chats' are in French" is valid but thin. In addition to validity, the interpretation should contain elements that make it, if not necessarily completely verifiable, at least falsifiable. Falsifiability must appear not just in terms of some evidence not yet discovered but also in terms of present evidence. In other words, the interpretation must be debatable in terms of its own evidence, and there must be some considerations that may count against it. The task of the interpreter is to anticipate these considerations—for instance, by rebutting possible counterarguments.

Again, nothing in this language about validity and falsifiability would make it necessary to believe, as Hirsch concludes, that there is only one meaning of a text and one corresponding understanding. Hirsch's notion of "correctness" in interpretation goes much farther than is necessary in order to give a theory of *validity*. It indicates that he has not perhaps overcome the initial confusion of validity and verification. He gives up the latter notion in order to grant the point that an interpretation is only probably correct at best and never completely certain. He writes, nevertheless,

This distinction between the present validity of an interpretation (which can be determined) and its ultimate correctness (which can never be) is not, however, an implicit admission that correct interpretation is impossible. Correctness is precisely the goal of interpretation and may in fact be achieved, even though it can never be known to be achieved. We can have the truth without being certain that we have it, and, in the absence of certainty, we can nevertheless have knowledge —knowledge of the probable.   [*VI* 173]

His claim that an interpretation can be true without the interpreter's knowledge sounds metaphysical insofar as it suggests that there is some object or entity (for instance, a thing-in-itself, or the ultimately correct interpretation that can never be apprehended) that exists behind the veil of our perceptions and finite understanding in such a manner that we can make claims about it—possibly correct claims—without knowing it. If knowledge of the truth is impossible, the claim that "the truth has in fact been achieved" has no real use; it is merely empty or, in both the ordinary and the philosophical sense of the term, dogmatic.

Under analysis, then, Hirsch's new intentionalism does not yield any new, positive practical consequences. On the contrary, it has a negative practical consequence in that it can potentially lead to a hardening of the interpreter's beliefs in the correctness of his own readings of a text to the exclusion of other readings. Given this result at the practical level, and conceptual unclarity at the philosophical level, it becomes important to challenge the theory and to offer a positive alternative.

III. MEANING AND CONSCIOUSNESS

The essential weight of Hirsch's intentionalism rests on a philosophical rather than a practical issue. His position puts him at odds with the anti-Cartesian philosophy of language found, although in very different styles, in both the Heideggerian hermeneutics of Gadamer and the Wittgensteinian anti-intentionalism of Wimsatt and Beardsley. Hirsch feels that both these positions are misconstrued, since meaning can never be derived from the text alone, being the result of the author's intentional consciousness permeating and animating the words. The text has meaning, he argues, precisely because meaning is something that comes out of a consciousness.

> If there is a single moral to the analyses of this chapter, it is that meaning is an affair of consciousness and not of physical signs or things. Consciousness is, in turn, an affair of persons, and in textual interpretation the persons involved are an author and a reader. The meanings that are actualized by the reader are either shared with the author or belong to the reader alone. While this statement of the issue may affront our deeply ingrained sense that language carries its own autonomous meanings, it in no way calls into question the power of language. On the contrary, it takes for granted that all meaning communicated by texts is to some extent language-bound, that no textual meaning can transcend the meaning possibilities and the control of the language in which it is expressed. What has been denied here is that linguistic signs can somehow speak their own meaning—a mystical idea that has never been persuasively defended.   [*VI* 23]

This passage makes it possible to expose a clear disagreement with Hirsch and thus to enter into genuine philosophical debate. The question is whether, if one still wants to talk about an intention in the language of the text, one has to attribute this intention to a person. It may be possible to speak in a more limited way of the intention of the text itself. In interpretation the notion of intention is useful; it is necessary to have a sense of the whole in order to understand the parts, and the notion of intention captures the way the parts are tied to an overall whole. The word "structure" is also sometimes used in this sense (although more recent linguistic structuralism uses it differently).

To argue that it is valid to speak of the intention of a text, and not necessarily of a person, it must be shown that Hirsch's attempt to connect meaning with consciousness is not particularly useful. On the contrary, the notion of consciousness is extraneous. Though simple argument will not necessarily persuade an adamant intentionalist, who will want proof in a stronger sense, it will convince those who want a theory that is useful while eliminating unnecessary hypotheses.

Several considerations are involved in the inference beyond the text to an intending consciousness. The traditional notion of intention involves a view whereby the meaning of what is to be said exists before the actual saying (as "design" or "plan" or even goal). Thus the utterance attempts to "express" a meaning or thought, which in turn is what the saying *intends* to say (although the actual utterance can fail and say something different). On this view language is almost always inadequate. Just as language about a feeling fails to do justice to the actual feeling, so language about the thought is inadequate to the range of implications of that thought.

That inadequacy is built into language may be true, but not for the reasons implied by the doctrine of intention. The reason for the inadequacy is not the inaccessibility of something external or neutral to language. Rather, the inadequacy is a function of language itself insofar as it is a self-enclosed but always open-ended system. Utterances take place in time, and the range of implications of an utterance may become apparent only later—with, for instance, the specification of implicit, unexpressed anterior conditions. The inadequacy of language may be explained in ways that differ from traditional, psychological intentionalism without accepting the hypothesis that language-independent or language-neutral entities are subsequently brought into language.

The issue under discussion is not specifically whether there is a subjective language that is "private"—that is, accessible only to the subject in whose mind the language occurs—but more generally whether the claim that "meaning is an affair of conscious-ness" indeed explains anything, whether it has any actual *use*. Does the claim that meaning is an activity of "consciousness" really say anything at all? In the *Investigations* Wittgenstein asks, "Whom do I really inform, if I say 'I have consciousness'? What is the purpose of saying this to myself, and how can another per-son understand me?"[14] One purpose of talking about "conscious" meaning may be to note that the interpretation of my utterance by the other person does or does not match what I had "in mind" or "in my consciousness." On the other hand, the other inferred his meaning from my language. Is it true, then, that the meaning is something I had "in my head" but may not have expressed well? What imparts sense to my words if not my meaning? Such an in-ference, Wittgenstein points out, is "a dream of our language" (*PI* par. 358). Why is it a "dream"? I certainly have the experience that what was said does not totally express what was meant to be said. But then, what *was* "meant" to be said? What was "there" *before?* A meaning? An intention? Did I experience something in my consciousness that I did not experience in my actual saying?

Breaking down the notion of "experiencing something in my consciousness" to its components, the first question concerns what it means to experience "consciousness" (*PI* par. 418). The notion of consciousness already contains the idea of experiencing, and an experience of experiencing is an illusion based on objectify-ing what actually goes on. Bringing an object into consciousness is not bringing the object into relation to another object: conscious-ness is not a thing. Similarly, meaning is not a thing. If we think the meaning of a word is something we experience, we may believe that intention is something located in our heads and only inci-dentally found in the locution. Alternately, we may develop the notion that in inferring the intention from the words, we are find-ing out what the other person "experienced." Yet is this a mean-ingful model? Wittgenstein says, "Call it a dream. It does not change anything" (*PI* 216). In trying to find out what is meant by the words, Wittgenstein suggests that we look at the way the words are used, not the way the use itself is "experienced."

But didn't I already intend the whole construction of the sentence (for example) at its beginning? So surely it already existed in my mind before I said it out loud!

—If it was in my mind, still it would not normally be there in some different word order. But here we are constructing a misleading picture of 'intending,' that is, of the use of this word. An intention is embedded in its situation, in human customs and institutions. If the technique of the game of chess did not exist, I could not intend to play a game of chess. In so far as I do intend the construction of a sentence in advance, that is made possible by the fact that I can speak the language in question.   [*PI* par. 337]

Language is not a phenomenon that is experienced; rather, it has the same logical status as notions such as consciousness and experience, since it signifies the mode in which particular phenomena appear. Language makes possible something like intention, and not the reverse. On the other hand, "language" is not an unembodied phenomenon; it manifests itself only in particular situations. When someone talks about language, he is talking about use; and use, roughly, precludes bringing in the notion of consciousness. On this point R. Rhees is quite right when, writing against A. J. Ayer on the possibility of inventing a private language, he notes,

It is possible, certainly, to invent new expressions, and even in one sense new languages. But it is a different question whether anyone could have invented language. If language were a device or a method which people might adopt, then perhaps he could. But it is not that. And you could as easily speak of someone's inventing commerce; more easily, in fact. For he would have to invent what we call use and meaning. And I do not say so much that this would be beyond anyone's powers as rather that it is unintelligible.[15]

This argument is not new, for it contains many of the nineteenth-century objections to the idea of accounting for the "origins" of language. But it does show that the logical status of the notion of language is not the same as the status of notional objects in the world. It may be said that the appearance of language is simultaneous with the appearance of the world. In another sense, of course, language is only one part of the world, and the two senses must be kept distinct. The idea that language takes its "meaning" from the life that is breathed into the signs by the "consciousness" of actual persons confuses these two notions of language. An experiential proposition is confused with a grammatical one, making the former extraneous.

The peculiarity of this confusion of a grammatical sign with an experiential content is concisely pointed out by the *Investigations,* paragraph 432: "Every sign *by itself* seems dead. *What* gives it life?—In use it is *alive*. Is life breathed into it there?—Or is the *use* its life?" The notion of a consciousness breathing meaning into the linguistic signs, which Hirsch says are "dead" by themselves, is thus as extraneous as a hypothetical but unobservable beetle in a box. As long as the word "beetle" has a use—indicating that which is "in" the box—the "meaning" of the word lies in its use, not in its connection to the external thing (see *PI* par. 293). The *experience* of the meaning of the word or the consciousness that gives life to dead linguistic signs are useless theoretical constructs.

Wittgenstein's arguments here do not claim that the notion of intention is in itself nonsensical. There are cases where it is valid to inquire after the intention—as in the law court, for instance, where the intention can be inferred indirectly from various observed facts, and it can be correctly concluded that "he intended to rob the bank" (*PI* p. 214). Similarly, there is no doubt that speech can also perform acts, and these acts have a meaning that is not confined to the meaning of the words. A child's statement that he is hurt can just as easily be a request for sympathy as a real report of pain. But the word "meaning" can have a different sense, depending on whether it is applied to the meaning of the act or the meaning of the words, and these senses should not be confused. The meaning of the act willed by the author (both as a biographical person and as an artist) may be to create a literary work of art that is a self-contained whole. This intention does not, however, affect the meaning of his words—nor should it, for the work should be autonomous by his very intention. The work could then be said to have its own, internal intentions.

Contrary to what Hirsch believes, it does make sense to speak of the intention of text, and especially of the intention of the literary text or the poem. In order to learn how the parts of a picture, for example, fit together, the picture must be seen as a whole in its pictorial form. The intention of the text is like the pictorial form. Accordingly, Wittgenstein's statement in the *Tractatus* still holds: "A picture cannot, however, depict its pictorial form: it displays it" (2.172). The intention is thus not something different from the poem, nor does it "accompany" the poem. It *is* the poem. Yet it is what the poem shows, not just what it says. That is why people often look beyond the text for the *author's* intention: they have not yet seen what is being shown.

Speaking about the intention of the text has the potential theoretical advantage of avoiding the traditional vocabulary of Cartesian philosophy of consciousness and hence the antinomies of subject-object language. Wittgenstein's philosophy, as well as Heidegger's, has this force. Once the appeal to the consciousness of the author is eliminated, however, other questions remain, including how the intention of a text is determined by the interpreter. One answer is provided by the hermeneutic theory of Gadamer, who argues that the text takes part in an interpretive *dialogue*.

TWO

The Nature of Understanding: Hans-Georg Gadamer's Philosophical Hermeneutics

Hermeneutic philosophy takes seriously the question of establishing the conditions for the possibility of acquiring historical knowledge of past culture. Heidegger's reformulation of the notion of essence allows for a way of thinking of humans as beings that are essentially historical rather than defined by an unchanging essence. Man's being, which is not fixed forever in an eternal *eidos*, is a function of the way he sees himself in time and in a particular historical situation. The ontological primacy thus given to human historicity in Heidegger's and Gadamer's hermeneutic philosophy determines the approach to the question concerning the nature of historical knowledge. A generation will not only understand itself differently from the way a past generation understood itself, it will also understand that past generation differently from the way the past understood itself.[1] Since a central element of any generation's self-understanding is a picture of its place in history, subsequent historical actualizations will radically alter that image. For the old generation's hopes, fears, and indefinite adumbrations, the new generation can substitute knowledge and hindsight. Correlatively, the cultural achievements of one age will appear differently to a subsequent age than to an even later one. We do not see Plato as Descartes or as Kant saw him, but we certainly see Plato differently because of Descartes and Kant. Gadamer's hermeneutics insists that the effect, or *Wirkung*, of a text is an important con-

stituent of its meaning. Since this *Wirkung* differs for different
ages, it has a history and tradition—what Gadamer calls a *Wirkungsgeschichte.* For a contemporary interpreter this history is
still operant, moreover, since his own understanding of the text
grows out of and is conditioned by it. The uniqueness and importance, as well as the difficulty, of Gadamer's hermeneutics is
found in this description of understanding and the conditions
under which it evolves and changes.

Objectivists reject the hermeneutic notion of "understanding
differently" on the grounds that it would be impossible in principle to understand past ages and cultural achievements objectively—that is, free of the values and norms of the present age. Of
course objectivism can be formulated as a mere attempt at understanding the past age as it understood itself. Such a formulation,
however, is too general. No historical analysis is content to stop at
the self-understanding of the past. Its aim is to know whether such
self-understanding involves fundamental distortions. Both the so-
called historicist hermeneutic position and the objectivist position
can claim access to the self-understanding of the past. The real
quarrel centers on whether the present perception of the past age's
self-distortions is itself distortion-free. The claim to distortion-
free perception is implicit in the objectivist's rhetorical question to
the historicist whether it is ever possible to understand past ages or
past texts "truly." The historicist appears unable to deny consistently that a "true" understanding exists. The denial that something has been understood truly at least seems to imply that there
is something that has been understood falsely and that could eventually be understood truly. The skepticism of the "radical historicist" would thus be inconsistent.

Whether or not Gadamer's hermeneutics can legitimately be
labeled "radical historicism," it has certainly been attacked under
this rubric by other hermeneutic theorists, such as Betti and
Hirsch. The objections to Gadamer raised by Hirsch represent
some of the usual criticisms of historicism and provide a conveni-
ent example of the objectivist reaction to a philosophy that makes
historicity its fundamental principle. Behind these objections lies a
sharply divergent understanding of the task of hermeneutic theory
as such. This divergence must be made clear in order to understand
the philosophical scope of Gadamer's thinking.

I. TWO CONFLICTING CONCEPTIONS
OF HERMENEUTICS

Hirsch's basic criticism of Gadamer points out that radical historicism, like any philosophical skepticism, is a doctrine that cannot
be proved or disproved; it is merely a dogma, a matter of mysterious faith (*VI* 44). In raising this claim the objectivist is on shaky
ground himself, for just as it cannot be proved that there has *never*
been a true understanding, so it is impossible, Hirsch admits, to
prove that texts have in fact been truly understood. Proof would
require all the evidence and this completeness eludes a finite
observer. The notion of proof is too strong, ignoring the point
that positions that cannot be proved in this sense can nevertheless
be backed by good reasons—in fact, by reasons that are better
than those given for other positions.

This belief in the inability of the historicist to prove his claim
empirically must be modified into a demonstration of why radical
historicism is *probably* false. Hirsch offers two major arguments.
He claims, first, that historicist hermeneutics does not properly
distinguish between the need for reevaluation of the past age by
the present one (given the new interests and needs of the present)
and the need for understanding the past age in and of itself. That
is to say, the *subtilitas intelligendi* and the *subtilitas explicandi* are
confused to such an extreme that the past age is lost forever. It can
only be perceived through the distorting perspectives of an ever-
changing present. Hirsch protests that this result fails to cohere
"with the rest of experience" (*VI* 257), for he contends that some
communication between past and present has been experienced.
This apparently benign appeal is turned into a rhetorical argument
when he further claims that if communication has ever occurred,
understanding of the past must be possible and radical historicism
improbable (*VI* 257).

Stated in this way, Hirsch's argument is not particularly convincing. The appeal to the distinction between the *subtilitas intelligendi* and the *subtilitas explicandi* is inappropriate, since the
cogency of this very distinction is challenged by historicists, and
especially by Gadamer, who wants to rethink the entire traditional
notion of understanding. Furthermore, the appeal to the coherence with the rest of experience allows his potential opponent to

point out that experience also supports the idea that literary texts of past ages are understood differently by different ages. There is, in fact, intuitive evidence for both historicism and objectivism.

Hirsch's first objection, therefore, cannot be persuasive, for the appeal to normal intuitions works both ways. His second major objection is more nearly based on a matter of principle. If the gap between past and present is indeed as radical as historicist hermeneutics contends, Hirsch argues, no understanding, not even of texts in the present, is possible. Hirsch explores this thought in two ways. First, he questions what constitutes the "present," claiming that each moment can be said to be different; thus, the notion of people being in the "same" generation or speaking the "same" language is an "illicit abstraction" (*VI* 257). Second, Hirsch pushes this *reductio* argument further by arguing that the gap between persons is as great as between ages: "Differences of culture," he thinks, "are manifestations of this root possibility of differences among men" (*VI* 257-258).

Hirsch's claim that the historicist uses the term "present" in a vague manner is well taken. The historicist obviously appeals to a camel's-back notion of the present as a broad period of time wherein a great deal can take place. In shifting to a razor's-edge notion of the present, however, Hirsch has not eased the problem. If the present is too narrowly defined and reduced to an immediate instant, it becomes impossible to see the unity of the historical event in the plurality of its subinstants.

The part of Hirsch's objection that is more illuminating because it reveals a fundamental difference of attitude is the priority he gives to differences among persons over differences among cultures. Hirsch is here adopting a typical objectivist position called "methodological individualism" when it is used in debates on philosophy of history. This view, derived from Karl Popper's attack on Marx and Hegel around the time of the Second World War,[2] insists that individuals rather than groups (for instance, classes) are the moving agents of historical events and therefore the proper basic unit of historical explanation. The alternative, "methodological holism," exists in several varieties, depending upon the interpretation of the holistic unit. Gadamer's writings may sound like a version of methodological holism, since he argues that historians and literary critics are conditioned by the tradition in which they stand; they cannot escape the fact that the history (Wirkungsgeschichte) of the effects of the text or past culture is still operant in determining the questions they raise and the paradigmatic problems they try to solve.

That such a view sounds Hegelian, however, does not mean that it is adequately described by the label "holism" or historical "determinism"—the fatalistic element in holisms which methodological individualists find most dangerous. To accuse Gadamer's hermeneutic theory of such a deterministic holism is to forget the important influence of Heidegger on Gadamer. Since the very starting point of Heidegger's "fundamental ontology" is the investigation of individual human existence, it would be a serious mistake to consider Heidegger a holist. Heidegger's philosophy makes no claim to discover a necessary progress in history. Similarly, the hermeneutics of Gadamer is not making claims about the content of "history" (both in the sense of historical occurrences and of historiography). The real question concerns describing the conditions of the interpreter's or historian's understanding. One of these conditions is the source of the understanding in a *situation.* Since Gadamer's reflection on the *Wirkung,* or conditioning effects, of history does not lead into a speculative philosophy of history or even into a theory about the kinds of causes or principles behind historical events, it is not a form of determinism. On the contrary, his reflection leads to a call for greater self-reflection on the part of the historian or literary interpreter, for an increased self-consciousness about the influence of background and tradition on present thinking and research.[3]

The objectivist will not be satisfied, however, to know that hermeneutics allegedly of the historicist stamp is committed neither to methodological individualism nor to methodological holism. He will also want assurance that, in addition to the increased self-reflection demanded of the interpreter by Gadamer, it is possible to eliminate successfully all the prejudices and distortions forced on the interpreter by his tradition and situation. Gadamer himself holds that self-reflection cannot be complete (*WM* 285). The major issue, then, continues to center on the threat of relativism. It points to an additional underlying difference—a divergence in the very conception of what hermeneutic theory is and what it needs to explain.

The fundamental conflict between an objectivist hermeneutics such as Hirsch's and the more "historicist" hermeneutics of Gadamer rests in the fact that the former sees the relation to the text as a *knowing* relation, whereas the latter is concerned with a description of the nature of *understanding* as such. Accordingly, the former poses the problem of generating a theory of textual understanding in a way different from the latter. The objectivist must deal with the problem of preventing a breakdown or collapse in the relation between text and interpreter. The antidote appears to lie in finding a point of view, a stance from which to see the object —that is, the literary work—in proper perspective. Visual metaphors become important, and the question of the *propriety* of the perspective and the *correctness* of the account become the central theoretical concerns. The goal—seeing the object clearly—is furthered by the means of finding a method or a definite theoretical criterion against which the interpreter's insights can be measured. The general assumption, then, postulates a definite object (a single meaning) present in the work. The only further question consists in determining how much we, the knowers, can know.

The considerations raised by the historicist intend to show that the hermeneutical problem cannot be so narrowly defined. The reflection on the "babel of interpretations"—the modern proliferation of methods and materials—must make hermeneutics more "restless" by opening up disquieting questions. What happens when the object of interpretation disappears, when it fractures and splinters so that we begin to suspect that our own eyes are multifarious? What happens when the suspicion arises that the scientific horror peering back up at us from the analytic microscope is our own eye?

Such suspicions become particularly acute when the cultural product being interpreted is a literary work. The notion that an interpretation is a knowing relation with an object begins to suggest why the status of the literary work's meaning is unclear. All three terms—"knowing," "relation," and "object"—do violence to the nature of the literary text. "Relation," suggesting that two "things" are to be brought together, already specifies a distance and a distinctness between the text and the reader; the text is posited as an "object" existing at a distance from a subjective consciousness that must reach out to it. Such a description, however, does not concur phenomenologically with the process of actually reading a literary work. Rather, the immediate experience is closer to a fusion of the reader into the text.

Against the objectivist presupposition that the literary art work is a distant pole of a subject-object relation, Heidegger, in his essay, "The Origin of the Artwork," proposes a different ontological account of art. For Heidegger, the work of art is not an object—that is, something projected by a subject. His alternative account shows that something can *claim* us when we see it and not just "appear" to us or be simply and *indifferently* "there." A work of art is precisely that about which we cannot be indifferent. It is not a tool that disappears into its use—that is, not a means for arousing in us an "aesthetic experience." On the contrary, it is a *work,* and it continues to claim us because it transcends any context we try to impose on it. Moreover, the claim shows itself in that the artwork conditions our very understanding of ourselves, our time, and our situation. Thus, the artwork is historical not in being a moment *in* history, but rather in being a condition for or even a generating force of subsequent cultural achievements.

Gadamer's own theory of art in the first part of *Wahrheit und Methode* continues in the general spirit of Heidegger's attempt to rethink the phenomenon of understanding art. The consequence of this aesthetics for hermeneutic theory is that it requires a better description of self-understanding before assuming a definite set of epistemological categories and problems based on the model of a knowing relation between subject and object. Traditional hermeneutics from Schleiermacher to Hirsch is concerned with the knowing relation, and specifically with the problem of preventing misunderstanding of texts (see *WM* 173). The task of Gadamer's ontological hermeneutics is more fundamental in that it raises questions about the very possibility of coming to understand at all.

An ontological hermeneutics, such as Heidegger's and Gadamer's, does not rule out questions of "truth" and "validity," but it puts them at a different remove and in a different perspective. Dealing with these questions involves "translating" from their ontological theory of understanding into more traditional epistemological language. Such a translation (to be attempted in the later parts of this book) must take into account that knowledge is not quite the same phenomenon as understanding. There is a clear difference between the questions, "Do you know the poem?" and "Do you *understand* the poem?" It is possible to know the poem in the sense of being able to recite it and even give a lot of facts about it. But these are not tantamount to understanding. Knowledge generally reduces to factual assertions, while understanding implies something "more." Though this "more" may seem vague in comparison with the cognitive explicitness of assertions, it nevertheless consists of very real aspects of experience. Without them, factual assertions often lose their force, for they include the sense of the whole, the overview with its myriad adumbrations, associations, and connotations that remain in the background and yet determine whether the emphases and import of a text are properly grasped.

An objectivist may continue to think that this emphasis on the "more" of understanding makes Gadamer's philosophical hermeneutics noncognitive and subjectivist. In the subsequent explication of the details of Gadamer's notion of understanding, it will be necessary to show that the position is not just a mystical dogma and that the "more" can be specified. Gadamer's analysis clearly draws on such important cognitive elements in the philosophical tradition as Aristotle's concept of *phronesis* and supports itself with a wealth of reasons derived from the lessons of philosophical experience.

II. THE LIMITS OF OBJECTIVITY

What motivates the expansion of hermeneutics from a *Kunstlehre,* a code of the canons of proper interpretation, into a distinctive philosophy? When Heidegger entitles his famous lecture "What Is Metaphysics?" he provides Gadamer both with an example and an explanation of this expansion. The stress in the question should be on the middle word—what *is* metaphysics?—emphasizing the obscurity, and possible falsity, of the present understanding of the subject matter. "The meaning of the question 'what is metaphysics?' " writes Gadamer, "is to ask what metaphysics really is in contrast to what it thinks it is or to what it would like to be."[4] Understanding is not always a straightforward case of confronting a clearly delimited subject matter and assembling all the proper information. In order to understand something like metaphysics, *interpretation* is required. There is a difference between coming to understand a metaphysical text, or a solution to a particular problem in a metaphysical system, and coming to understand metaphysics as such. In the latter case, we must ask why metaphysical questions are raised and what it means to do metaphysics (with the awareness that asking about metaphysics in this interpretive way can itself be metaphysical). The more fundamental a question, the more it demands that the self-understanding of the question be itself examined and interpreted.[5] The "truth" of the resulting interpretation goes beyond being a function of the correctness of the information used in the interpretation. A more important consideration is whether the interpretation is itself productive or not, whether it opens up new dimensions of thought and new lines of inquiry.

The criteria for judging an interpretive understanding differ from those that apply to a deductive explanation. Examples of this process drawn from Heidegger's philosophical exegeses may not themselves be good examples of sound scholarship, and it is too early to judge their productive force. A different example, found more persuasive by other hermeneutic philosophers,[6] is the practice of psychoanalysis. The interpretation offered by the analysis can seldom be proved objectively true or false. Its "truth" lies rather in its power to deepen the patient's self-understanding, opening up a new realm of self-perception. The interpretation verifies itself for the patient through its productivity in leading to therapy and cure.

Psychoanalysis thus provides an example of a kind of understanding best described as an inquiry in which the objectivity of the interpretation cannot be determined independently of the value or use of the interpretation. Indeed, the ideal of an "objective fact of the matter" is a less appropriate criterion in this case than is a notion such as "increased, or more productive self-understanding." An objectivist theory of understanding insisting on an "objective fact of the matter" thus fails to give a very enlightening account of the phenomenon of understanding in the process of psychotherapy. A hermeneutic philosophy of the nature and conditions of understanding cannot limit itself to those strict natural sciences in which objectivity is a more obvious feature and more rigorous conventions establish what counts as the fact of the matter. It must also take into account those areas of thought where correctness of interpretation cannot always be clearly ascertained apart from such other considerations as the productivity or heuristic value of the interpretation.

Even in the case of the stricter sciences, the notion of objectivity cannot be assumed to be self-evident. The Freudian suspicion of the surface of consciousness is paralleled by a similar suspicion of the apparent objectivity of science when science is considered as a social institution. A common Marxist criticism (which can be developed much more subtly, of course) argues that scientists, especially in the social sciences, who think themselves neutral and objective are in fact operating under social conditions in such a manner that their apparent disinterestedness actually reflects social interests.[7]

The same criticism may be expressed in non-Marxist terms by pointing out that objectivity in these sciences depends on accepting certain paradigms (typical problems, methods, measuring devices, and the like) tied to a particular tradition. Even though these may not be the only possible or plausible paradigms, they can be claimed to be preferable precisely because they are bound to a tradition. Entrenchment in a scientific tradition can be as important a criterion for preferring a theory as is theoretical simplicity. The connection with the tradition may, for instance, increase its heuristic value.

To approximate this idea to Gadamer's terms, we can say that the kind of questions raised in the particular sciences (whether physics or philology) is a function of the *Wirkungsgeschichte* in which the inquiry takes place. A valid reason for preferring a particular line of inquiry is its connection with a tradition. Furthermore, in many cases increased self-consciousness about these connections with the tradition will increase the productive value of the findings.

The knowledge attained by scientific inquiry is thus tied to a particular self-understanding by the sciences which is itself an interpretation that cannot be confirmed by the same kind of objective proof possible within the inquiry itself. Hermeneutic theory that attempts to go beyond objectivism thus does not necessarily do away with objectivity. Gadamer's intention is clearly not to

weaken scientific objectivity (that is, to question the scientific findings) but only to show its limitations (see *WM* 517-518).

The purpose of Gadamer's hermeneutical philosophy, then, is
to describe the activity of understanding in general and not to provide an epistemological philosophy of science or a logic of scientific explanation. This philosophy wants to describe not only the
understanding of a particular subject matter but also the self-
understanding of the inquiry, which conditions the questions
asked and hence the conclusions.

An adequate account of understanding in this way requires the
investigation of a broad range of "sciences" and especially a
choice of those in which understanding and interpretation are particularly observable. Gadamer himself does not deal with psychoanalysis. Rather, he focuses on the humanistic sciences, especially
history, jurisprudence, and philology. For Gadamer's philosophical hermeneutics, the interpretation of literary texts is the most
paradigmatic of these. The need to describe adequately the encounter with art provides him with a basis for going beyond a narrow definition of truth as the assertion of facts. Literary art, furthermore, has a priority over visual art, since, in Gadamer's view,
all understanding ultimately takes place in language.

The broadness of Gadamer's concerns will not, of course,
reduce the importance of questions about the possibility of objectivity in interpretation. In order not to distort the phenomena,
however, these questions must follow a fuller description of understanding.

III. UNDERSTANDING, INTERPRETATION,
AND APPLICATION

It is no accident that the terms "understanding" and "interpretation" have been less clearly distinguished in the discussion of
Gadamer than in the analysis of Hirsch. A fundamental principle
of Gadamer's theory holds that the separation of understanding
and interpretation is only an abstraction. "Alles Verstehen ist
Auslegung," insists Gadamer repeatedly (see *WM* 366, 373, 377);
all understanding includes interpretation. This point follows from
the necessary situatedness (Situationsgebundenheit) of under-

standing. Because an understanding is rooted in a situation, it represents a point of view, a perspective, on what it represents. There is no absolute, aperspectival standpoint (a contradiction in terms!) from which to see all possible perspectives. Interpretation is necessarily a historical process, continuously elaborating on the meanings grasped in an understanding and on the meaning of this understanding for itself. In this respect understanding is not a mere repetition of the past but participates in present meaning (*WM* 370).

Furthermore, there is no "one right interpretation" ("keine richtige Auslegung 'an sich' "—*WM* 375). Interpretation involves continual mediation of past and present. For literary interpretation in particular, Gadamer holds that interpretation of the text cannot in principle be limited merely to what the author intended or how his own time understood him. The text is not an expression of the subjectivity of the author (*WM* 372-373). Rather, the text only comes into real existence in a dialogue of the interpreter with the text, and the situation of the interpreter is an important condition of the understanding of the text.

The contrast between these hermeneutic views and more traditional ones is indeed quite striking. Hirsch thinks that Gadamer's dialectical blending of the *subtilitas intelligendi,* the understanding of the text, and the *subtilitas explicandi,* the explication, forces Gadamer into logical difficulties:

Attempting to efface this distinction results only in logical embarrassment before the simplest questions, such as "What does the explicator understand before he makes his explication?" Gadamer's difficulty in coping with this basic question is quite apparent when he comes to describe the process of interpretation. He cannot say that the interpreter understands the original sense of the text, since that would be to disregard the historicity of understanding. He cannot say, on the other hand, that the interpreter understands his own subsequent explication, since that would be patently absurd. [*VI* 253]

If these were the only two possibilities, then indeed Gadamer's theory would be incomprehensible. Is, however, the process of understanding adequately described by dividing it into two moments—an initial *intelligere* and a subsequent *explicare*?

The discussion of the limits of objectivity makes the naïveté of this reduction suspect. Arriving at the initial understanding can only be the result of a clarification, not only of the internal features of the text but also of the interpreter's own understanding both of the subject matter and of his own interpretive input. This input is constituted by various historical factors, including the tradition in which the interpreter stands, the historical accumulation of previous interpretations (conditioning, for example, what the interpreter thinks is new in his own reading), and the contemporary "state of the science" (the aims, methods, themes, and so on, currently in use). Gadamer claims that these factors can never be completely eliminated from the understanding of the text per se; they can only be made more or less clear. The critic who ignores these factors in his understanding is being not more but less objective.

Hirsch's failure to recognize the situatedness and historicity of understanding is evidenced in his review of *Wahrheit und Methode* (*VI* 245 ff.). He omits all discussion of what Gadamer characterized as "the central problem of all hermeneutics," the problem of the *subtilitas applicandi* (see *WM* 290 ff.). Historically speaking, the *subtilitas applicandi* was considered a third moment of understanding, along with the *subtilitas intelligendi* and the *subtilitas explicandi*. It can be found, for instance, in such Pietists as J. J. Rambach (*Institutiones hermeneuticae sacrae,* 1723). With the complete fusion of *intelligere* and *explicare* by the Romantics, however, the moment of *applicatio* is obscured. Thus the *subtilitas applicandi* is of little importance to Schleiermacher and later thinkers and is ignored by Hirsch. Schleiermacher's hermeneutics, which involves preventing misunderstanding, sees interpretation as a subject-object relation in which all that is strange in a text is to be made familiar. Thus, distinct problems of application disappear once the gap between text and interpreter is bridged by this familiarity. The use to which the achieved understanding could be put, as in a sermon (in the case of theological hermeneutics) or a legal judgment (in the case of juridical hermeneutics), would follow self-evidently.

Gadamer himself, of course, does not want to revert to a position whereby the three moments are completely distinct. He argues, rather, that application is an integral part of *all* understanding. Just as "understanding is always interpretation [Auslegung]," similarly, "understanding is always already application

[Anwendung]'' (*WM* 292). The literary interpreter is thus in a very similar position to the theatrical director staging a drama or to a judge in a law court handing down the verdict. The literary text, the drama, and the law code all stem from earlier periods, and there are usually precedents for their interpretation. Since the present situation is never exactly the same as the situations of the previous interpretations, however, even the judge cannot merely repeat a precedent. In order to be just, he, like the others, has to reinterpret the history of precedents in terms of the new factors in the present context.

The importance Gadamer attaches to the *applicatio* is thus a function of his central principle that understanding is grounded in and constituted by a concrete, temporal-historical situation. It would be a mistake, however, to misconstrue Gadamer's point as implying that the interpreter merely reads his own meanings into the text or that he only understands the text's meaning *to him* (not in itself). The goal of interpretation can still be *intelligere,* the reconstruction of the questions that the text itself is an attempt to answer. But while it will not suffice for the interpreter to impose his own questions dogmatically on the text, the question to which the text is an answer will also pose further questions for the interpreter himself. The judge will not be able to limit himself to an overly literal reading of the law if he wants to promote justice. Nor will the literary interpreter be able to restrict himself to a strictly historical exhumation of sources and antecedents if he wants to understand the *literary* meaning of the text.

The *applicatio* that, Gadamer insists, is involved in understanding is not the same kind of application involved in traditional epistemology. The question is not one of applying concepts or theories to a practical situation or a series of observations. The term is not used, furthermore, in the sense of "applied sciences" or "technological application." Gadamer must explain how understanding occurs at all, not how understanding can be properly applied. Since understanding is always embedded in a situation, the problem is not one of fitting preconceived notions to a situation, but of seeing *in the situation* what is happening and, most important, what is to be done. The connection between understanding and *praxis* is, for Gadamer, a very close one. His notion of praxis is, however, not the modern notion: it goes back to, and stands in the

Wirkungsgeschichte of, Aristotle's philosophy. Gadamer can only be properly understood if the considerable influence of Greek philosophy on his thinking is appreciated. Hence the connection of understanding and praxis merits closer explanation in order to prevent modern misunderstanding.

IV. UNDERSTANDING AND *PHRONESIS*

The modern distinction between theory and praxis, thinking and doing, is itself more theoretical than practical. The distinction is highly abstract, depending on a sharp bifurcation rarely found in actual experience. A gap does occur, however, when reflection is compared with the physical activity involved in carrying out an action. The reflection never provides completely sufficient reason for the action. In fact, ordinary life provides numerous examples of action that does not concur with the antecedent reflective conclusion. It is frequently necessary to distinguish between the decision arrived at by reflection and the decision represented by the actual action. Nor is it irrational to resist doing or believing something that has been shown to follow syllogistically from other beliefs; although the deductive sequence p, and, if p, then q necessarily leads to q, modal considerations show that "believing q" does not necessarily follow.[8] The practical reasoning of ordinary life does not function in the same way as theoretical reason.

If the distinction between theory and praxis is made as sharp as that between theoretical reason and actual doing, their relation is necessarily paradoxical. The question becomes whether such an extreme antithesis actually characterizes praxis. The difference between practical and theoretical reasoning has already been suggested; the relation of action to *practical* reason (once we have a more precise understanding of it) may not be so paradoxical. Furthermore, the reflection that an *action* in itself can be described as rational or irrational suggests that the distinction is not so absolute. Thus, unless we are strict Platonists, we can speak of a rational action without necessarily meaning that the action is the conclusion of a complete and consistent reflection. We mean, rather, that the action represents an immediate grasp of what is necessary in and appropriate to a particular situation. Practical *perception* is involved. An action characterized by careful reasoning but lacking this practical perception may still be called irrational.

Praxis, in fact, involves a practical understanding that is not just pure reasoning but is inseparable from action as such. Practical understanding involves more than knowing the general rules that guide action. Thus, children often know the rules for playing a particular game (that is, they can recite them when questioned), yet they do not necessarily understand how to play the game. They often still lack the capacity, for instance, to carry through the action appropriately, perhaps because they misunderstand a notion such as "capturing a piece."

Clarifying the relation of understanding and praxis is an important task in Gadamer's hermeneutics, and his idea that application is implicit in all understanding plays a central role. Of course, Gadamer is not unique in seeing the essential situatedness of understanding and its inseparability from actions and practical interests. Ludwig Wittgenstein also emphasizes the way understanding is grounded in and constituted by the meaning contexts provided by forms of life. Nor does he think a sharp wedge can be driven between understanding and application. In the *Philosophical Investigations* he argues that understanding a rule is *at the same time* understanding how to apply it (see para. 202). For Wittgenstein, to learn a rule is to master a technique, and this can also be said to be true in Gadamer's account of understanding.

Gadamer's own attempt to show the ties between understanding and praxis is, like Wittgenstein's, intended as a corrective to the "theoretical" problem posed by the apparent philosophical antithesis between theory and praxis. Unlike Wittgenstein, however, Gadamer searches philosophical tradition for a more viable notion of praxis and finds it in Aristotle.

For Aristotle, Gadamer points out,[9] the difference between theory and praxis was not, as it is today, the difference between reflective thinking ("Wissenschaft" in a broad sense) and the application of this thinking—that is, between thinking and something else. On the contrary, for the Greeks the distinction concerns thinking itself, and specifically two different kinds of thinking: on the one hand, theoretical philosophy (with mathematics—the study of the unchangeable—as its ideal), and on the other, practical philosophy (the study of the changeable). For Aristotle praxis is, in fact, not the antithesis to *theoria,* since *theoria* is itself a form of praxis.[10] When praxis is discussed specifically in terms of the status of free citizens in the *polis,* this is only one sense of the term, although the most eminent one. Most generally, it is applied to the whole range of life (bios) and to man as the only creature manifesting *prohairesis,* the ability to prefer and choose cogitatively. The task of practical philosophy is to bring this distinctive characteristic of man to consciousness, so that in the actual practice of preferring or discriminating men can be properly cognizant of the relation of their preferences or discriminations to the Good.

Gadamer holds that his own philosophical hermeneutics is akin to Aristotle's practical philosophy. Both involve general thinking, but the generality is restricted by the need for relevance to practical concerns. The praxis that concerns Aristotle in the *Nicomachean Ethics* is moral action, and the praxis that concerns Gadamer is interpretation (not just of texts but also of experience and world orientations). What hermeneutics and practical philosophy (in the Greek sense of a philosophy of praxis) have in common is a reflection on the essence of different forms of action. Without paradox, both center on the theory of praxis.[11]

There is an even deeper connection between Gadamer's philosophical hermeneutics and Aristotle's practical philosophy. Not only is Gadamer's self-understanding of the nature of his philosophy drawn from Aristotle but Gadamer's analysis of the nature of understanding is also grounded in Aristotle's ethics. The *Nicomachean Ethics* is concerned with the problem of the role of reason in action, and specifically in moral action. The notions of reason and action are not to be conceived too abstractly, however; otherwise there will be no way to mediate between them. Aristotle's criticism of Plato's notion of the Good—for Gadamer the nucleus of Aristotle's philosophy—is precisely that it is too general and abstract, and that it exaggerates in identifying virtue and knowledge, *arete* and *logos* (*WM* 295, 491). Aristotle gives a description that revises radically the Platonic account of the relation of the general and the particular and that is truer to the phenomenon of moral action. The originality of this description comes from its discovery of a cognitive capacity distinct from *episteme*—namely, *phronesis.* This distinction must be made clear if Gadamer's theory is to be understood, for he explicitly maintains that much of what Aristotle says of *phronesis* is true of understanding in general.

Phronesis (practical wisdom) combines the generality of reflection on principles with the particularity of perception into a given situation. It is distinguished from theoretical knowing (episteme) in that it is concerned, not with something universal and eternally the same, but with something particular and changeable.[12] It requires experience as well as knowledge. In this sense it is like the knowledge of a craftsman (techne), except that people do not have control over themselves and their destiny the way artisans have control over their product. Furthermore, practical wisdom differs from *techne* in that "while making has an end other than itself, action cannot; for good action itself is its end" (1140b 6).

Though practical wisdom is not purely reflective or purely intuitive, it is nevertheless a state, Aristotle notes, "by virtue of which the soul possesses truth by affirmation or denial" (1139b 11 f.). Not intuitive, it involves the reasoning of "deliberation"; hence, Aristotle specifically distinguishes it from intuitive reason, "for intuitive reason is of the limiting premises, for which no reason can be given" (1142a 25). Nor is this deliberation to be identified with the theoretical reasoning leading to scientific explanation and demonstration:

Now no one deliberates about things that are invariable, nor about things that it is impossible for him to do. Therefore, since scientific knowledge involves demonstration, but there is no demonstration of things whose first principles are variable (for all such things might actually be otherwise), and since it is impossible to deliberate about things that are of necessity, practical wisdom cannot be scientific knowledge nor art.   [*Nicomachean Ethics,* 1140a 32-35]

Practical wisdom is not reason pure and simple but involves a kind of perception—not sense perception (of colors, sounds, and the like), but a "perception akin to that by which we perceive that the particular figure before us is a triangle" (1142a 25-30).

Gadamer's concept of application is very similar to the notion of *phronesis,* since it too does not mean applying something *to* something, as a craftsman applies his mental conception to the physical material, but is rather a question of perceiving what is at stake in a given situation. Unlike *techne,* the craftsman's art, which possesses a teachable knowledge, practical wisdom cannot be taught. Nor is practical wisdom purely a reasoned state, for "a state of that sort may be forgotten but practical wisdom cannot" (1140b 30). For Gadamer, understanding is like *phronesis* in that it is a matter not only of reflection but also of perception and experience. The phenomenon of practical wisdom shows that in understanding in general, thought and action (or, in hermeneutical terms, the *subtilitas intelligendi* and the *subtilitas applicandi*) are not completely separate moments but are dialectically united in the very act of understanding.

Gadamer elaborates this dialectical structure of understanding by developing the idea that understanding and experience are inseparable. In order to argue this point, however, he first has to strip the concept of "experience" of some misleading connotations stemming from the Cartesian tradition.

As Gadamer uses it, "experience" (Erfahrung) is not in opposition to cognition in general, but only to explicit, self-conscious reflection (and particularly to *Reflexionsphilosophie* and Hegel). In this sense, understanding is itself experience. Accordingly, Gadamer speaks of the activity of interpreting the past as "the hermeneutical experience." He means to suggest that in the actual process of interpreting the tradition (Überlieferung), the tradition is *experienced* not merely as something over and done with but as something still important for the present (see *WM* 340-344). In other words, whatever the interpreter thinks about his activity when he stops interpreting and reflects on the nature and use of his interpretation, in the actual encounter with the text he is confronting meanings that are *present* meanings insofar as they make sense to him.

To clarify the scope of the notion of *Erfahrung* (which goes beyond the normal range of the English term "experience" and is therefore better left untranslated for the moment),[13] Gadamer gives an interesting analysis of Aeschylus' use of the phrase "to learn from suffering." Aeschylus, Gadamer argues, means to go beyond saying that failures and negative experiences can lead to wisdom and to the right course of action. Though the platitude normally suggests this message, Aeschylus means to show the ground for the truth of the saying.

What man should learn through suffering is not this or that, but is rather the insight into the limits of human existence, the insight into the insuperable barriers to the divine. . . . Experience [Erfahrung] is, therefore, the experience of human finitude. [*WM* 339]

In the most authentic sense, to experience means to know that one is not oneself the master of time and the future. This insight leads the wise man to greater openness both to the vicissitudes of life and to the reality of his actual situation.

The negativity so essential to the understanding arising out of *Erfahrung* distinguishes it radically, Gadamer believes, from theoretical knowing (the *Wissen* of *Wissenschaft*). The ordinary assumption is that learning from experience leads to increased knowledge and self-consciousness. Gadamer resists this conclusion, largely because he feels Hegel peering over his shoulder. Gadamer has learned from philosophical experience that this line of reasoning can result in the positing of an absolute knowledge. In Gadamer's view, Hegel's *Phenomenology of Spirit* develops the dialectic of experience in such a way that experience itself is overcome, transformed into the absolute self-consciousness of philosophical *Wissenschaft* (*WM* 337-338).

Gadamer, intent on preserving the insight into the finitude of human existence, finds his model in the emphasis on situatedness in Aristotle's notion of *phronesis* (as well as Heidegger's notion of facticity—see *WM* 511). Instead of thinking of *Erfahrung* as a coming-to-self-consciousness, as Hegel does, Gadamer sees it as resulting not in greater knowing (Wissen), but in an *openness to more experience* (*WM* 338). In this way Gadamer retains the negative moment of the dialectic—the principle of dynamic change—without being forced to accept the belief that a dialectic involves necessary progress. In thus preserving as a central principle the negativity of *Erfahrung* (the recognition of the finitude and historicity of man—that is, of his necessary situatedness), Gadamer prevents the escape into a false theoretical self-certainty and into methodological dogmatism.

Openness for the other also includes the recognition that I must let something in myself count against myself, even if there were no other who would make it count against me.... The hermeneutical consciousness [das hermeneutische Bewusstsein] has its completion not in a methodological self-certainty, but rather in the same readiness for experience that distinguishes the experienced person from one who is dogmatically constrained.   [*WM* 343-344]

Certainly Gadamer's insistence on the openness to more experience and the recognition of finitude is praiseworthy for exposing

the self-deception of dogmatism. The further question is, however, whether this openness can serve as a criterion for judging the
results of understanding and interpretation. If openness is to be
distinguishable from mere weakness of will, there must be some
explanation not only of the tolerance of understanding, but also of
its truth. Although understanding is always grounded in a situation, it also attempts to rise above that situation in order to say
something true about it. Gadamer has not failed to analyze this
movement of understanding toward language. In fact, his notion
of the linguisticality (Sprachlichkeit) of understanding, developed
from the Greek notion of the *logos,* is his most original contribution to the history of hermeneutics.

V. UNDERSTANDING AND LANGUAGE

In Gadamer's terminology the specifically *hermeneutical* experience is that which involves the experiencing of the tradition (Uber-
lieferung). This experience is, however, not limited solely to historians or philologists; it can be a moment in all interpretive understanding. In speaking of the hermeneutical encounter with tradition, Gadamer is not raising the particular epistemological question about the means of securing knowledge of the past. Such a
question presupposes that the past is an object standing over
against a knowing subject who gathers data about it from texts.
Gadamer analyzes the more immediate phenomenon of the very
communication of meanings through texts. "Tradition," Gadamer writes, "is not simply an occurrence [Geschehen] that one recognizes through experience and learns to control, but is rather *language* [Sprache], which is to say, it speaks from itself like a 'thou'
[Du]" (*WM* 340). The tradition, far from being an object, is more
like the other person in a dialogue.

Gadamer's description of hermeneutical understanding starts
from an analogous phenomenon, the I-thou (Ich-Du) relationship
(*WM* 340 ff.). This starting point is highly significant, for it indicates once more that the notion of understanding is not to be reduced to the epistemological relation between a subject and an
object. This analogy tempts us to say that there is a subject-subject
relation involved. The suggestion is misleading, however, because

Gadamer's "subject" is not a Cartesian "mind," an *inner* subjectivity that in some mysterious way has to see into the inner subjectivity of an external Other. On the contrary, Gadamer's theory presupposes Heidegger's analysis of *Dasein* as being-already-in-the-world. In hermeneutic experience what is being analyzed is the act of communication, and the participants exist in a world of previously shared meanings; that is to say, they share a language. In contrast to earlier, more psychological hermeneutic theories, Gadamer's contribution is to insist that hermeneutical understanding is "not a mysterious communion of souls, but rather a participation in a shared meaning" (*WM* 276).

Of course it is possible for an individual to treat another person as an object. In fact, the I-thou relation is commonly cast into this form. Gadamer analyzes three such derivative forms and shows their corresponding states in hermeneutical experience. In this first form a person is classified according to type-ideas about other people. The other person is subsumed under common psychological generalizations, truisms about human behavior, and types of personalities in much the same way that past events or literary works can be treated not as unique but as merely representative of more general and typical features of human behavior (*WM* 341). This first mode obviously forgets the role of the classifier in the act of classification. The classifier stands aloof from what is being analyzed, taking the objectivity of his classification for granted.

A second form of the I-thou relation is more reflective than the first and recognizes that, just as the I who classifies the Other would not find himself adequately described by such categories, so is the Other in fact not adequately treated by such knowing. The subjectivity of the Other, it is recognized, is not captured but remains radically other. This recognition of the otherness of the Other has as a correlative the hermeneutical experience of the radical otherness of the past (*WM* 342). Gadamer labels this second form of the hermeneutical experience "the historical consciousness." It does not subsume the past under general laws but recognizes the otherness of the past epoch and treats it as historically unique. This "historical consciousness," which describes much of the thinking about history in the nineteenth century, is inherited from Romanticism.

For Gadamer this second form has shortcomings similar to

those of the first form and must be criticized and superseded. The "historical consciousness" also forgets its own role in its understanding of the past, failing to see that to postulate the radical otherness of the past is to assume that the present knowledge is historically unconditioned and absolute. To posit the past as a closed matter that can be totally described (and its uniqueness confirmed) is to posit the present as having complete mastery and the last word over the past. This second form thus generates the objectivism of such historians as Ranke.

A third form of hermeneutic experience, unlike the previous forms, does not treat the past either as an object classifiable into properties or as a radically other time with values that the present can no longer share. Rather, it lets the tradition speak to the present and realizes that this speaking is telling the present something about itself. Gadamer calls this form "das wirkungsgeschichtliche Bewusstsein" (*WM* 343), a practically untranslatable term, meaning the consciousness of standing within a still operant history (Wirkungsgeschichte).

This consciousness, or self-consciousness, is most properly hermeneutical. It can best be understood by analogy with the corresponding form of the I-thou relationship. It is also the most authentic form: it neither treats the other person as an object or a means nor tries to master the Other by suspending his right to meaningful statement. (Gadamer is consciously drawing on Hegel's famous analysis of the master-slave relationship.) On the contrary, one is *open* to the other person for what he has to say. Without this openness, Gadamer argues, there can be no real human contact: "to belong together [Zueinandergehören] is always at the same time to be able to listen to each other [Auf-ein-ander-Hörenkönnen]" (*WM* 343). This does not necessarily mean that one must believe uncritically everything the other person says. In fact, out of respect for the other person one has an obligation to think through what is said as thoroughly as possible.

Understanding is always a form of dialogue: it is a language event in which communication takes place. *Hermeneutical* understanding is a language phenomenon in the further sense that the cultural tradition (literary, political, juridical, or the like) is itself present largely as "language" (in a broad sense of the term) and often as written texts. To interpret these texts is to come into dia-

logue with them. Understanding occurs, then, in the medium of
language: it is characterized by what Gadamer calls linguisticality
(Sprachlichkeit). Hence Gadamer's hermeneutic theory departs
from previous hermeneutics by avoiding the necessity of finding a
"bridge" for the gap between past and present, between text and
interpreter. There is no longer a need to posit some third term,
such as psychological empathy, in order to provide a common link
between two otherwise closed-off periods of time (or, in the case
of the literary author and the reader, between two subjectivities).
Past and present, text and interpretation, are part of an ongoing
language process. Meanings evolve and form a *Wirkungsgeschichte* in which the present interpretation itself stands and to
which it contributes. "The linguisticality of understanding,"
Gadamer writes, "is *the concretion of the hermeneutical consciousness* [wirkungsgeschichtlichen Bewusstseins]" (*WM* 367).

The *Wirkungsgeschichte* is not the *object* of hermeneutical
understanding, then, but the language, the medium, in which the
understanding occurs. To have a language is to be in a world,
Gadamer argues in connection with Humboldt's claim that a language or a linguistic outlook (Sprachansicht) is already a world
outlook (Weltansicht) (*WM* 419). While this unity of language and
tradition may solve traditional hermeneutical problems about the
bridge over the hermeneutical gap, however, it also creates new
problems of its own. For one thing, how is the interpretation going
to distinguish its own language and world outlook from that of the
historical past or literary text that it interprets? Gadamer himself
explicitly says that "the interpretive word is the word of the interpreter and is not the language and lexicon of the interpreted text"
(*WM* 448). Furthermore, the emphasis on the historicity of language (the connection of language to a historical world and world
outlook in such a manner that language is the carrier of the ongoing history of effects, the *Wirkungsgeschichte*), raises again the
problem of historical relativism. Gadamer explicitly states that
"each appropriation of the tradition is a historically different
one" (*WM* 448). Will Gadamer's "linguistic turn"—his turn
toward language and away from traditional subject-object psychology—enable him to avoid traditional relativism?

This question can only be answered by a step-by-step examination of various points of Gadamer's theory. The first step is to

make sure that his notion of linguisticality as dialogue is properly understood. Texts cannot, of course, *prima facie* be a partner in dialogue in the same sense that people can. The notion of interpretation as dialogue with texts may therefore have the relativistic consequence that the interpreter's dialogue with the text is merely a dialogue with himself, reducing dialogue to an inner monologue with no external checks on its validity.

Gadamer draws his analysis from the Platonic notion of dialogue, and especially from Plato's actual practice in writing dialogues. In this respect it is important to note that rational procedure and the pursuit of truth are clearly the goal of genuine discourse in the Platonic dialogues, at the same time the subjectivity of the interlocutors is not neutralized. Indeed, it is only insofar as the interlocutors come to agreement that the dialogue can proceed and draw closer to the truth.

The protagonists of the dialogues, then, are not just incidental; their personalities and circumstances are essential to the achievement of any positive accomplishment. Socrates himself makes a similar point in the *Gorgias* in speaking to Callicles, a person of peculiar importance to Socrates. Callicles, the man of action, is the exact opposite of Socrates. This contrast makes their confrontation more significant, however, for if two interlocutors who are, in the beginning of their dialogue, most in opposition can come to genuine agreement on the subject matter, then truth is more likely to have been established. The result itself will not be prejudiced by hidden, shared prejudices and by the subjective inclinations of the participants to agree for ulterior reasons.

The Platonic dialogues move first to break down preformed opinion (doxa) so that true questioning can proceed unbiased. For this reason Socrates' partners in dialogue are very often not the older and more famous thinkers who are set in their ways but younger students who are assumed to be more open to the true course of the *logos,* since they are less encumbered with doctrine.

Furthermore, if the truth of the dialogue is to shine through, the discourse must not be colored by the subjective dogmatism of the leader. The openness to truth entails the famous attitude of learned ignornace, called in medieval times by Cusanus, for example, the *docta ignorantia.* A stance of ignorance is adopted in an attempt to undercut unquestioned prejudices built into the education. The leader of the dialogue, if he is really questioning after the truth, cannot yet know the truth; the dialogue will transcend his own knowledge and be guided by the *logos* itself. Thus Gadamer can conclude that genuine dialogue precludes subjectivism: "What emerges in its truth is the *logos,* and this is neither yours nor mine, but rather exceeds the subjective opinion of the partners in the discussion to such an extent that even the leader of the discussion always remains the ignorant one" (*WM* 350). Gadamer goes on to argue that subjectivism is also precluded in genuine dialogue by the priority of the phenomenon of "hearing" (citing Aristotle's *De sensu* 473a 3 and *Met.* 980b 23-25; see *WM* 438 f.). Unlike seeing, where one can look away, one cannot "hear away" but must listen, unless the language is an alien one or is mere chatter. Even idle chatter has a way of captivating the listener against his will. Hearing implies already belonging together in such a manner that one is claimed by what is being said. Meaning is not arbitrarily construed, and a message is heard as a statement of something in particular and not merely anything at all.

The *docta ignorantia* has the effect of averting the threat of dogmatism at the same time that the concern for a genuine dialogue oriented toward the subject matter acts to ward off a relativism that would be introduced if the subjective opinions of the interlocutors were at stake. The subjectivity of the interlocutors is still at play in the dialogue, since each interlocutor must come to see the truth for himself in his situation. The interlocutor must examine himself in order to be open to the transcendent truth of the subject matter. The enterprise is not to justify something already chosen, decided upon, or evaluated, but to lead toward and make possible a decision, choice, or valuation.

The phenomenon of Platonic dialogue is, of course, changed when, rather than being present at the scene, one only reads or hears about it. Plato himself criticized writing for destroying the natural, dialectical movement of thought. Does this point undercut Gadamer's assertion that the dialectic of hermeneutical understanding of written texts is like a dialogue? One must remember that some of Plato's dialogues are themselves only reports of debates that occurred elsewhere. More significantly, however, Plato himself *wrote* dialogues. While he may be criticizing the kind of writing that hides behind the dogmatic deafness of the sophistically written word, he is also demonstrating that writing itself can produce the original movement of genuine discourse. Although Platonic dialogue requires at least two speakers, the reason is embedded in the dialectical nature of dialogue itself and not in the rhetorical need for the presence of two characters to mouth the ideas. The fact that many of Plato's protagonists debating with Socrates are merely yes-men does not indicate, at least for Gadamer, a failure of the art. The phenomenon of such ready agreement demonstrates a necessary condition for the attempt to let the subject matter develop *itself,* without interference from the individuals' *opinions.* Dialogue cannot be just a question of persuasive rhetoric and self-gratification in the winning of arguments. The purpose is not to win arguments but to seek the truth (*WM* 349).

Accordingly, in hermeneutical understanding a text can also be brought into dialogue if the interpreter really attempts to follow what the *text* is saying rather than merely projecting his own ideas into the text (*WM* 253). The meaning of the text is in *one* sense the meaning given by the interpreter, since the text poses a question to him in his particular historical situation and he approaches the text with given expectations. But in a larger sense it can be said that the projection is a function of the text itself, for the interpreter can test his expectations against the text. The meaning of the text can claim the interpreter only insofar as it comes from beyond him and transcends him. In a sense the text does speak; that is, it shows a meaning that claims our attention by addressing us in a manner relevant to our concern with our particular situation. As part of our own tradition, for instance, the text is constitutive of our situation in such a way that we cannot remain indifferent to it. At the same time it also holds interest for us because it is an address from a perspective other than our own. If we did not experience the text as other, if we experienced it as merely something of our own invention or something completely familiar (Schleiermacher), we would not be caught up by and interested in the text. It would have nothing new to say to us. Furthermore, if the "text" were really nothing more than a monologue with ourselves, it would not grasp our attention. If we find that we are merely listening to our own ventriloquism, we lose interest in *what* is being said or lapse into admiration of the sheer sound of our own cleverness.

Just as in dialogue where the partners are not merely interested in each other but in the subject matter of the discourse, so in reading texts one is claimed by what is said, by the subject matter (Sache). This emphasis on the *Sache* is an essential aspect of hermeneutical understanding, and Gadamer follows Heidegger in attaching central importance to it.

Understanding always involves upholding the opinion that is to be understood against the power of the meaning dispositions that rule the interpreter. This hermeneutical exertion is required precisely when we are claimed by the subject matter. Without being claimed by the subject matter, one would not be able to understand the tradition at all. What would result is the total indifference to the subject matter by the merely psychological or historical interpretation that enters there where one actually no longer understands.   [*WM* 473]

The distance between the interpreter and the text is not the distance between a subject and an object, since the text has already entered into the meaning horizon of the interpreter. Insofar as the text can address the interpreter, it comes to him as something to be understood and to be brought into dialogue on a subject matter at hand.

VI. BEYOND RELATIVISM?

Dialogue is the attempt to attain a true understanding about a subject matter. The concern of understanding with a subject matter and the experience of the meaningfulness of the interpretation in this regard is the sign of the moment of *applicatio* in understanding. The very intention of claiming that understanding is at the same time interpretation and application is precisely to avoid relativism. This intention can now be made clearer in the light of the analyses of *phronesis* and dialogue.

Certainly the humanistic, historical disciplines would be in severe straits if interpretation came down to saying "this is what the text means *to me*." There would then be no grounds other than personal preferences or contemporary fashions for disputing different or conflicting interpretations. Yet not all positions short of absolutism are committed to such a radical relativism, and in order to avoid oversimplifications, stronger and weaker formulations must be distinguished.

In the case of relativism, two positions may serve as a start, after which it will be possible to add further refinements. The question is whether a position can be formulated in such a way as to be at least rational enough to be seriously plausible. There is a weak sense of relativism whereby saying "the text means such-and-such" only means "it means this *to me*" or "*I like* it read this way." In contrast to this *subjectivistic* kind of relativism, which results in an impossibility of agreement through rational discourse, it is easy to formulate very generally another position that does not lead to such irrationality. This version can be called *contextualism,* for according to it, the interpretation is dependent upon, or "relative to," the circumstances in which it occurs—that is, to its context (particular frameworks or sets of interpretive concepts, including methods). For contextualism, rational reflection and dispute do not stop with the interpreter's personal preferences. On the contrary, although the choice of the context for an interpretation is underdetermined by the evidence, justifying reasons for the appropriateness of that context rather than alternative ones can and should be given. Since no context is absolute, different lines of interpretation are possible. But this is not radical relativism, since not all contexts are equally appropriate or justifiable. Contextualism denies that there is an objectively neutral first step providing an unquestionable methodology. This general position is not properly called relativism because it is held by both relativists and nonrelativists.[14]

Hence arguing that interpretations are relative to the historical-cultural situation of the interpreter is not *necessarily* relativistic. Contextualism demands justifying reasons for interpretations, and these reasons can be assumed to be as factual or "objective" as any an objectivist could produce.

Of course the fact that the choice of the context for an interpretation is underdetermined means that the framework for the interpretation cannot be justified as completely as can particular "facts" within the interpretation. Nevertheless, the choice of context or framework is far from arbitrary. When Gadamer speaks of the hermeneutical experience, he is describing the practice of actual interpretation. The interpreter does not consciously choose a certain set of interpretive concepts to be "applied." When Gadamer links application to linguisticality as the medium in which the interpretive understanding arises, he is suggesting that the interpretive concepts disappear in the very coming-to-appear of the text's meaning. The interpretive concepts are not necessarily consciously thematic, and the interpretation is not a second meaning accompanying the initial understanding (*WM* 375).

Gadamer's version of contextualism thus holds that the interpretive understanding is conditioned by preunderstandings (Vorverständnisse) arising out of the situation of the interpreter. These preunderstandings can be made conscious by the interpreter insofar as he wants to defend the appropriateness of his understanding and to justify the legitimacy of his interpretation. But since such self-reflection can never lead to clarification of all the preunderstandings, all interpretation must remain partial and contextual. Can the interpreter paradoxically believe both that his interpretation involves true insight and that it is partial and conditioned?

Philosophers like to say that the discovery of a philosophical paradox is not the end of the matter; it is what first makes things interesting. Of course no unnecessary paradoxes should be raised —but Gadamer does not believe that his position is paradoxical. A paradox might be involved if in asserting the conditional character (the situatedness) of all understanding, he also believed that assertion to be itself unconditional. However, he consistently argues that

Even when we ourselves, as historically enlightened thinkers, are fundamentally clear about the historical conditionedness of all human thinking and hence about our own conditionedness, we have not ourselves taken an unconditioned stand. ... The consciousness of the conditionedness does not in any way negate this conditionedness.   [*WM* 424; see also *WM* 505]

There is no unconditioned standpoint, not even for philosophical hermeneutics.

Gadamer's reflection on conditionedness takes a similar turn when he addresses the notions of linguisticality and historicity. Although all understanding takes place in language, "the linguistic experience of the world [die sprachliche Welterfahrung] would not be able to take a standpoint outside of itself in order to see itself as an object" (*WM* 429). There is no way to see language from a nonlinguistic viewpoint. Similarly, man is a being involved in an ongoing history, and there is no way he can get out of history to view history as a whole.

Again for Gadamer the model for a philosophy simultaneously affirming rationality on the one hand and facticity and human finitude on the other is provided by Aristotelian ethics. Gadamer concludes an essay entitled "On the Possibility of a Philosophical Ethics" by noting:

Aristotle can thus recognize the conditionedness of all human being in the content of his theory of *ethos* without it being the case that this theory denies its own conditionedness. Only a philosophical ethic that in this manner not only knows of its own questionableness but also actually has this questionableness as its essential content seems to me to be adequate to the unconditional character of the moral.					[*KS* I 191]

The task of the practical philosophy of Aristotle, it has been argued, is to take into account the changeable character of man. Yet to talk about changeability is not to make the relativistic assertion that everything about man is conventional or arbitrary. There are, for instance, natural rights. Though the notion of natural rights suggests that there are unchanging aspects of man's existence, Gadamer points out that for Aristotle unchangeable natural rights could belong only to the gods. For man even what is true by nature—as, for instance, that the right hand is stronger than the left (a favorite example of Plato's)—can be changed, as by training the left hand (*WM* 302 ff., 490 f.; *KS* I 191). The natural is not merely conventional or expedient. Like the best state, however, which is everywhere "one and the same," it does not, Aristotle says, have to be the "same" everywhere in the sense that the fire burns the same in Greece as in Persia (*WM* 302-303).

Gadamer concludes that the force of Aristotle's notion of natural rights is in no way dogmatic, since natural rights may vary. Rather, the idea has a critical or regulative function: it represents a valid point to which to appeal *at a particular time and place* when one right conflicts with another. Gadamer believes that all man's concepts of his ideal self serve a similar function. These ideas are more than conventional, since a "nature of the matter" (eine Natur der Sache) is implicit in any situation. This nature of the matter (for example, the ideal of courage) can only be determined within the situation itself, however. It is not a fixed ideal, and norms are not, for Aristotle, "written in the stars." But neither are norms merely conventional and relativistic. An ideal is only a

schema that is first made concrete in the moral-political situation
—that is, in the confrontation with the demands of actual practice
(*WM* 301-302).

For these reasons, then, Gadamer does not think that his ontological notions of the facticity (situatedness), historicity, and linguisticality of understanding entail philosophical relativism or
nihilism. Gadamer is not just presenting an ontology, however,
but is also developing a hermeneutical theory of interpretation.
This ontological hermeneutics must be tested critically against the
specific demands of hermeneutic practice itself, and particularly
against the practice of literary interpretation. The challenge is to
see whether his hermeneutical philosophy can avoid paradox and
at the same time allow for the possibility of rational discourse
about conflicting interpretations. Can a hermeneutic theory do
justice both to the recognition of the historicity of interpretation
and to the experience of truth in understanding?

THREE
Text and Context

In that precisely the poet with the pure tone of his original sensibility feels himself grasped in his whole inner and outer life and takes a look around at his world, just so is this new and unknown to him: the sum of all his experience, his knowledge, his intuition, his memory, art, and nature as shown in him and outside him —everything is as if for the first time, and hence present to him as indeterminate, unconceived, dissolved in pure matter and life. And it is especially important in this instant that he take nothing as given, that he start from nothing positive, and that nature and art, as he had earlier learned and sees them, do not *speak* before a language is there for *him*.[1]

This passage from Hölderlin presents reasons for resisting the reduction of poetry to ordinary discourse or even to fiction. Clearly, the poet believes that poetry does not depend upon pre-established meanings for its force. Familiar expressions and ordinary usage must be suspended if poetry is to see and make us see things "for the first time." Poetic truth is not derivative from ordinary truth—it is even possible that the latter is derivative from the former. Nor are we to suppose that ordinary usage has to do with truth and falsehood, while poetic usage is a collection of potentially false statements simply not asserted as true. Poetry does not try to be a predication; rather, it suspends both ordinary predications and the ordinary world as such, since it posits a completely new world. According to this view, poetic language is its own ground; it functions without recourse to an encompassing, external reality or to everyday language. Poetry transcends these dimensions and is essentially reflexive.

If poetry is self-referential as the passage suggests, the situation leads to important philosophical questions. From our more ordinary, everyday perspective, in which language has meaning only insofar as it communicates information and is about something in particular, it is difficult to understand how poetic language can *refer* to anything, how it can have "aboutness." Can poetry, like Lewis Carroll's Humpty-Dumpty, make words mean anything it wants them to mean? Is its interpretation equally arbitrary?

The hermeneutical theory of interpretation as described thus far deals more directly with the latter question than with the former. Yet this strategy of beginning with the nature of understanding is not without import for the theory of poetry, and for traditional questions of aesthetics. Gadamer's *Truth and Method* itself begins with a long discussion of the history of aesthetics and only develops the distinctly hermeneutical theory toward the end. To think of the hermeneutic theory of interpretation as a narrow part of aesthetics would, however, be misguided. Hermeneutical philosophy grows out of a dissatisfaction with the failure of aesthetics to transcend its perpetual dilemmas, its quarrels about whether to define art in terms of distinctions between sense and intellect, emotion and cognition, delight and deliberation, mediacy and immediacy, concreteness and abstraction, mimesis and expression, or truth and beauty. Hermeneutics is not a part of aesthetics, but on the contrary, aesthetics will in a certain sense be a part of hermeneutical philosophy.

This inversion may seem counterintuitive, especially if it is supposed that the interpretation of texts can begin only after the standards for aesthetic judgments have been established in an appropriate theoretical way. There is a long, sophistic tradition of raising the rhetorical question, how can one even select a work of art for interpretation before knowing what art is? The question implies that practice is impossible without first having a theory. Is it not more intuitive, however, to think that theory evolves cut of practice and will itself evolve as practice refines and modifies itself? Practice influences what emerges as theory, and theory in turn can then influence practice.

To capture the sense in which Gadamer's program goes beyond both traditional hermeneutics (as method of exegesis) and traditional aesthetics, it could be labeled a hermeneutical poetics. "Poetics" too, though, must then be freed from the narrow Platonic-Aristotelian sense of the term as the theory of poetry, where poetry is simply one artistic form among others. If poetics is considered as *poiesis* in the larger sense of "making" in general, then it is not so remote from practice, and from the practical philosophy discussed in the last chapter.

This connection of *poiesis* and practice even has a place in the English literary tradition. Thus, Ben Jonson (in *Timber*) attempts to distinguish poetry (the sum of an author's poems) and poesy (the practice in general). Jonson's notion of the practical as something more equivalent to "hard work" appears rather different, however, from the creative, originary *poiesis* described in the previous passage quoted from Hölderlin. The philosophical problem arising in both poets' theories about the genesis of poetry concerns the relation of ordinary and poetic language. Is poetic language radically distinct from ordinary language? Does each language involve its own form of truth as well as its own form of expression?

Philosophical hermeneutics does not begin with the question of the genesis of poetry as a particular craft, but with the question of understanding in general, and poetic understanding as a particularly difficult paradigm case. Poetry only comes to be in a process of understanding. Although this generalization holds for the poet, the critics are the ones who, in a reflective age like ours where there is more criticism than poetry, provide most of the data for an account of the process of understanding poetry. There is nothing backward about first providing a description of the conditions for critical understanding and then seeing what follows for some traditional theoretical quandaries about poetry and its truth. The hope—which the present book only begins to explore—is that such quandaries can eventually be dispelled by seeing how they arise from within the general process of understanding and why they are not problematic when rephrased from that point of view.

Gadamer's hermeneutical philosophy relies on an analysis of dialogue, and this analysis has interesting consequences for the distinction between ordinary and poetic language. Looked at sepa-

rately, poetry and everyday discourse do appear quite heterogene-
ous. Yet if they were entirely exclusive of each other, how would
literary interpretation be possible? Is the interpretive language
ordinary or poetic? For dialogue to be possible, there must be a
shared basis for communication. Dialogue is only interesting, however, if there is a distance and a difference both between the ques-
tioners themselves and between the questioning and that about
which one questions.

In this chapter Gadamer's notion of dialogue will be examined
in terms of its consequences for a theory of the conditions for the
possibility of literary interpretation. How does a dialogue determine its own boundaries? When does a dialogue with a text cease
being immanent or intrinsic and become transcendent or extrinsic?
A strategy of finding a context for the text may be essential to all
interpretation as a condition for the very possibility of interpretation. But how are we to determine whether a work will accept these
contexts? Art, as a corollary of the concept of aesthetic distance, is
said to be context-free. Even if a work will accept a context, what
are the boundaries of context? Are there contexts that are illegiti-
mately narrow or broad? These questions are important for the
methodology of criticism. The problem is to explain the interrelation between the tendency of interpretation to see language as
bound to a context and the tendency of poetry—as supposedly
self-referential, immanent language—to break free from established contexts even to the point of constituting a context uniquely
its own.

The intrinsic-extrinsic distinction for interpretive discourse is
tied to the distinction between poetic and nonpoetic discourse. If
the latter distinction cannot be maintained in a sharp and exclusive
way, then the former distinction will only be functionally relative.
Conversely, if practical criticism cannot supply the evidence that a
purely intrinsic criticism is possible, it becomes more likely that
the poetic-nonpoetic distinction really serves evaluative rather
than descriptive purposes. After determining the fate of the distinction between poetic and nonpoetic language, and between the
immanence of the poetic text and the contextual character of interpretive and ordinary discourse, the question of the truth of poetry
can be more readily clarified.

I. THE ESTRANGEMENT OF WRITING:
DERRIDA'S BOTTOMLESS CHESSBOARD

Is dialogue, and the speaking relation in general, an appropriate model for the task of generating a hermeneutic theory of poetic interpretation? Is dialogue only a metaphor for the process of interpretation, and a limited one because of the obvious difference between speaking and writing? In actual discourse, as opposed to written literature, the situation in which the speaking takes place supplies readily observable constraints on the interpretation of the meaning. The boundaries of the dialogue can be specified at any moment by one of the speakers, and if a remark is "out of context," it is often relatively easy to determine why.

These limitations on context are missing in important respects, of course, when the "partner" in a dialogue is a text. Can the text "tell" us when an interpretation is "out of context"? Is dialogue an appropriate model for the hermeneutic investigation of texts? Since the text is mute, it cannot be exactly analogous to a real partner in dialogue. The problem is even more acute when the text at stake is poetry. The central concern of some poetic texts is precisely with breaking down all previous ordinary understandings, all everyday contexts, and possibly any context whatsoever. To understand what supplies the context for a dialogue with a poetic text, the hermeneutic theory that interpretation is a dialogue must first be critically clarified.

The dialogue, according to Gadamer, is made possible by the condition of a preunderstanding (Vorverständnis) on the part of the participants. This preunderstanding extends not only to the participants' expectations in regard to each other's standpoint but also to an understanding of and concern with the subject matter (Sache) of the discourse. The fact that this preunderstanding conditions the discourse does not therefore make it subjective or relative in the sense that it is completely arbitrary, since the central concern is this subject matter itself. Nor does the existence of a preunderstanding make the dialogue dogmatic, for in genuine dialogue preunderstanding can be brought to consciousness and checked against its ramifications in terms of the subject matter itself. If the preunderstanding is shown to be inadequate, then the one-sidedness it introduces into the interpretation can be exposed, and the path will be opened for further interpretation. This is the skeleton of Gadamer's argument.

Gadamer's work represents one way of developing insights going back to Heidegger's *Being and Time* and drawing on such analyses as that of *Vorverständnis*. Since Gadamer's work appeared, another philosopher has also developed Heidegger's philosophy in a provocative and original way. Jacques Derrida's work represents a brilliant rethinking not so much of Heidegger's earlier thinking—the fundamental ontology and hermeneutic phenomenology influencing Gadamer—but of Heidegger's later, antimetaphysical writings. These later pieces by Heidegger point beyond a projected end of philosophy and of modern technological thinking toward a totally new beginning. Derrida is skeptical about the new beginning and often criticizes Heidegger for remaining trapped in the same metaphysical metaphors and strategies Heidegger himself rejects.

In many respects, however, Derrida and the later Heidegger share the same intention of exposing the Western metaphysical tradition by showing that its distinctions and metaphors only conceal an unexplained bias in favor of presence. Metaphysics has always given a privilege to presence whether in the form of the temporal present or in the form of intuitive presentations (as opposed to representations); it has always been, to use Heidegger's terminology, ontotheological since it has assumed that existence is justified only insofar as it is grounded in a being that is transcendent but nevertheless present. Derrida, like Heidegger, questions this absolute privilege of presence and, like Nietzsche and Freud as well, carries this critique against any philosophy (such as Hegel's or Husserl's, but also the scientific methodology of Saussure or Lévi-Strauss) affirming the self-assured certitude of consciousness. Insofar as Heidegger still resorts to such metaphors as "the call of Being," "the House of Being," or "the speaking of Being," however, Derrida suspects that Heidegger is still looking for a metaphysical key to unlock the secret meaning of Being, and thus, that Heidegger's own inclinations are still ontotheological. To counteract such inclinations Derrida offers another metaphor, that of a "bottomless chessboard"—a play that has no meaning beyond itself, no deep, underlying ground that supports it and speaks through it.[2]

The metaphysical prejudice in favor of presence is particularly manifest for Derrida in ancient and modern philosophical attitudes toward language. Language, indeed, is always at the center of Derrida's thinking. He conducts his negative transcendental arguments against unconscious metaphysical assumptions both in and through language, that is, both in his playful use of language and through his explicit analyses of language use. One of his more important and extensive analyses concerns the traditional epistemological and ontological priority given to speech over writing (l'écriture). Since Gadamer models his theory of understanding not only on the early Heidegger but also on Plato's dialogues, one must ask whether Derrida's criticism of the "Platonic" priority of speech would also be a criticism of Gadamer's use of dialogue as a hermeneutical paradigm. Does Derrida's analysis show Gadamer's notion to be merely a metaphor, and an inappropriate one for written texts? Or is it the case that Gadamer's and Derrida's views supplement each other because both thinkers are engaged in the same critical attack on metaphysical assumptions about truth, method, and absolute self-certainty? A short explication of Derrida's criticism of the priority of speech will help deal with these questions.

For Derrida the traditional priority of speech over writing represents a metaphysical bias that he attributes to the Platonism of the modern world-historical situation. He cites, for example, Plato's condemnation in the *Phaedrus* (277e) of the infantile play represented by writing, contrasting it with speech, which Plato considers serious and adult.[3] Unlike others, who attribute Plato's suspicion of writing simply to the fact that speech was just beginning to be written down in Plato's time and the process was not yet perfected, Derrida sees this suspicion as constituting a bias that has continued to the present day. The bias is especially noticeable, he argues, in the science of linguistics that, following Saussure's lead, construes writing as a mere derivation from speech.

Derrida's critique of Saussure in *De la grammatologie* is similar to his critique of Husserl in *Speech and Phenomena*. Both Saussure and Husserl, Derrida argues, are caught in a philosophy of presence, which aims to ascertain the presence of self to self. When this kind of philosophy turns its attention to language, it is bound to focus on speech, for speech seems to guarantee the presence of concrete objects in the meaning of the words of the speaking subject. The subjective self anchors itself in the world of objects through the referential capacity of language. The threat of meaninglessness seems overcome when perception and utterance are simultaneous.

But does speech guarantee this certainty? Derrida analyzes as an example the sentence, "I see now such and such a person through the window," at the moment I actually see him (*SP* 92 f.). Using an argument very similar to Hegel's demonstration of the poverty of immediate sense-certainty in the *Phenomenology,* Derrida objects to the ordinary realist assumption that discourse presupposes the possibility of intuitive presence. He argues that, on the contrary, in order to be understood, the sentence must have universal applicability and thus must presuppose the possibility of the *absence* of an immediate intuition. In other words, *because* I say the sentence, and *because* it can be understood by someone who does not have the perception I have, the meaning of the sentence must be part of the sentence itself and is not that particular intuition or perception.

Traditionally, writing is considered a later derivation of speaking, as the empty shell or husk of speech which has to be embodied by the intention of a consciousness to "live" again. Thus, writing represents the *absence* of a speaker, and speech the presence of a speaker. Attributing such a view to Husserl, Derrida sees a Platonic split between body and soul as suggested in the famous "cloak" analogy:

Writing [l'écriture] is a body that expresses something only if we actually pronounce the verbal expression that animates it, if its space is temporalized. The word is a body that means something only if an actual intention animates it and makes it pass from the state of inert sonority (Körper) to that of an animated body (Leib). This body proper to words expresses something only if it is animated (sinnbelebt) by an act of meaning (bedeuten) which transforms it into a spiritual flesh (geistige Leiblichkeit). But only the *Geistigkeit* or the *Lebendigkeit* is independent and primordial. As such, it needs no signifier to be present to itself.... Such is the traditional side of Husserl's language.   [*SP* 81; see *DLG* 52]

Although Derrida is not simply inverting priorities, he questions this traditional view by suggesting the interesting inversion that speech, rather than being anterior to writing, is derivative from writing. Writing, he thinks, is primordially absence; it presupposes the absence of the object and of the subject. But, he argues, speech also requires this absence; it requires an asymmetry, a difference, between intention and intuition, just as writing does. This asymmetry is linked to the fact that the proposition "I see so and so" has to be understandable by someone who does not have that particular perceptual presence. The intention of speaking is only accountable in terms of the possibility of this absence, not in terms of the intuition alone, for this presence would never give rise to the need to speak.

Derrida argues further that while the spoken term "I" seems to express the self-certainty of presence, it actually presupposes an absence since it has a universal application—that is, it would be understandable when uttered by any person in that situation. In fact, Derrida claims, this is the point behind the *ergo sum:* "When I tell myself 'I am,' this expression, like any other according to Husserl, has the status of speech only if it is intelligible in the absence of its object, in the absence of the intuitive presence— here, in the absence of myself" (*SP* 95). Derrida feels that Husserl, who holds the "I" to be personal, violates his own position in not recognizing that the word "I" is understandable even when its "author" is fictional or dead (*SP* 96-97).

Here again speech seems to embody the same conditions that characterize writing. Recent writers in France, including Maurice Blanchot and Roland Barthes, have been arguing that in writing the author, the "I," does not try to make himself present but, rather, is essentially absent.[4] Writing represents the death of the *I:* witness the tendency to treat works as if their authors were dead, even when they are alive, or the formalist tenet of intrinsic criticism as opposed to psychological reconstruction of the author. Such interpretive strategies can certainly be justified in terms of literary art, where the author, after all, desires his book to stand on its own merits. Blanchot has found the Orpheus myth to be especially significant in terms of literary writing. The artist has to descend into the blackness of Hades—that is, he has to face death and his own negation in order to make art possible.

The idea that writing is prior to speech is, however, radical, and perhaps more polemical than philosophical in intention. All that follows from Derrida's analysis is the *possible* absence of what is talked about. He himself recognizes that nothing in this thought forces us to give priority to the written sign over the spoken sign. In *De la grammatologie* Derrida suggests that his statement "language is first...writing [ecriture]" (*DLG* 55) requires qualifications. As a first scruple a footnote mentions that taking this priority to be a genetic one is "suspicious" (*DLG* 17). We may add that such an assumption is also obviously false: children learn to speak before they learn to write, and writing is a later development of any culture. Derrida recognizes, however, that his point is nongenetic and ahistorical (*SP* 103). Secondly, his definition of *écriture* is extremely broad, covering a wide range of phenomena from making marks on paper to painting, music, sculpture, sports, and so on (*DLG* 19).

The interesting feature of Derrida's notion of *écriture* is that, once the polemical rhetoric is seen through and the broad extension of the concept understood, it can be considered an important supplement to Gadamer's theory. For one thing, it makes us more wary of saying that the text "speaks" to its interpreters, a statement that otherwise may seem only metaphorical or too obviously true. Furthermore, his interpretation of the "speaking subject" as an absent "I" also adds an important subtlety that must be considered in any description of language. On the other hand, his account of the conditions of writing also extends to speaking. As a consequence, writing, in both a broader and a narrower sense of Derrida's technical term, can be said to communicate just as primordially as speaking. In other words, by rejecting the idea that writing is dead language that has to be brought to life by the intentions of the reader, by exposing the metaphysical prejudice involved in thinking of writing as a cast-off cloak, Derrida overcomes the objections raised against the idea of a dialogue with a written text. Hearing and reading are no longer so disanalogous, for hearing is also a kind of reading—an *interpretation* of the universality of the proposition in terms of the concreteness of the situation.

Undoubtedly Derrida's thought is considerably more radical

than Gadamer's, but there are also broader respects in which Derrida's critique of contemporary thought is not in disagreement with Gadamer. Despite the fact that Gadamer's main work precedes much of the French structuralist movement and Derrida follows it (through his very act of generating a "post-structuralist" critique), Derrida's critical attitude toward structuralism shows a greater compatibility with hermeneutical thinking than might be expected. In a key essay, "La structure, le signe et le jeu dans le discours des sciences humaines,"[5] Derrida discusses his disagreements with the structuralism of Lévi-Strauss. His main point reads like a gloss on Gadamer's ironical title *Truth and Method:* Lévi-Strauss goes in the right direction by separating truth and method, but he deceives himself in continuing to think that proper, rigorous method guarantees that his enterprise is objective and scientific (see *ED* 417 and 426 f.). Derrida agrees with Lévi-Strauss that there are no necessary truths, only interpretations, but he maintains that there are two different interpretations of "interpretation." One, that of Lévi-Strauss, is still caught in a metaphysics of presence and hopes that the study of primitive societies will show man his lost origins, the obscured deep structure of existence. Lévi-Strauss's nostalgia and his concern for scientific objectivity show that he has more ontological commitment to his structures than he would admit; he is still dreaming the dream of deciphering the fundamental order or truth of things.

The other interpretation of "interpretation," that of Derrida himself, is no longer romantically or nostalgically searching for the origins and foundations of thought, but is more Nietzschean in affirming that there is nothing more than interpretation, and that interpretation is only play (*jeu*). The notion of play is one that Gadamer also develops in the context of aesthetics, but Derrida uses it in a broader way, since the "bottomless chessboard" becomes a symbol for the search for meaning. And Derrida thinks that Lévi-Strauss is not courageous enough to recognize the Nietzschean insight that the play is bottomless or completely open-ended. Lévi-Strauss, through his belief in the objectivity of method, is trying to play it safe; he wants, Derrida believes, his game to be a sure thing, "un jeu *sûr*," by "limiting itself to the *substitution* of *present, given,* and *existent* pieces" (*ED* 427).

An essential feature of Derrida's notion of play is its open-endedness. In a sense the game being played on the bottomless chessboard is one that cannot be won. Of course, it may be necessary to try to win, although Derrida has not said whether this is so, but failure is always inevitable.[6] Derrida makes a similar claim about the attempt by Heidegger, Nietzsche, and Freud to destroy or overcome the history of metaphysics. The very attempt to destroy metaphysics uses terms inherited from the metaphysical tradition, and they, like the rest of us, remain imprisoned in the finitude of language.

Of course, in another sense, if one gave up the ontotheological notion of winning, of coming to a final completion, then one could also give up the notion of failure, and simply play for the sake of the play. Perhaps this is the Nietzschean affirmation. What is affirmed here is both the necessary imprisonment in language and the openness of language to new possibilities. Derrida's insistence on openness is similar to Gadamer's notion of openness as discussed previously in chapter two. Both Derrida and Gadamer reject the possibility and utility of projecting a totalization of experience. Gadamer wishes to avoid the notion of a Hegelian completion to experience (in absolute self-certitude) and the final end of history. Derrida argues that totalization is impossible not because of an empirical impossibility, but because of the finite nature of the game. "If totalization, then, no longer has any sense, this is not because the infinity of a field cannot be covered by a view or a finite discourse, but because the nature of the field— that is, language and a finite language—excludes totalization: this field is, in effect, that of a game (*jeu*), that is to say, of infinite substitutions in the closure of a finite ensemble" (*ED* 423). Gadamer too derives his notion of openness from finitude, and both thinkers insist on openness as an antidote to metaphysics, and especially to teleological or eschatological thinking, to the positing of a necessary order in the development of both history and thought.

II. IMMANENCE AND REFERENCE: RICOEUR'S HERMENEUTICAL ARCH

The hermeneutic model of interpretation as dialogue can be extended to cover written texts with no greater difficulties than arise in explaining communication between speakers. Traditionally, however, literary and poetic texts present special problems for aesthetically-oriented hermeneutics. There is first a question about appropriation: can these texts be legitimately appropriated into contexts of meaning extrinsic to the text itself? A correlative difficulty concerns the peculiar immanence of works of art: do poetic texts constitute their own, purely intrinsic context of meaning, or do they necessarily refer beyond themselves? Gadamer has not discussed the important question of the reference of texts in great detail, but one hermeneutical philosopher who has is Paul Ricoeur. Ricoeur attempts to synthesize structuralist concerns about the autonomy of texts with hermeneutical concerns about the contextual character of interpretation. In so doing he generates an account of appropriation and reference which deserves comparison with Gadamer. Many of Ricoeur's insights supplement Gadamer's work in valuable ways, but there are also important points on which the two hermeneutical theories diverge. Since there is much greater proximity in style and thought between Gadamer and Ricoeur than between Gadamer and Derrida, it is potentially more useful to highlight their differences rather than their considerable agreement.

That the "I" in writing is anonymous, that some poetic writing is without a specific context and may even destroy any particular context into which it is placed, often makes interpretation both necessary and impossible. Ricoeur has seen the important difference between the reference of speech and the estrangement or suspension of reference in the text. In his essay "Qu'est-ce qu'un Texte? Expliquer et comprendre"[7] he argues against the idea of interpretation as dialogue, possibly with Gadamer in mind, although the essay is basically an encounter with Dilthey:

In effect, the relation write-read is not a particular case of the relation speak-respond, it is not a relation of interlocution, it is not a case of dialogue. It does not suffice to say that reading is a dialogue with the author through his work; it is necessary to say that the relation of the reader to the book is of a completely different nature. Dialogue is an exchange of questions and answers; there is no exchange of this sort between the writer and the reader; the writer does not respond to the reader; . . . the reader is absent at the writing; the writer is absent at the reading.   ["QT" 182]

Like Derrida, Ricoeur distinguishes sharply between speech and writing; it is not his aim to make writing merely a derivation from speaking. Defending the autonomy of writing, he argues that writing is neither a reflection and fixation of an anterior speech, nor a translation of a speech act or a speech intention. Rather, it is a distinct phenomenon, the result of a direct inscription. For Ricoeur writing and speaking are equiprimordial, although he does speculate on whether the comparatively late appearance of writing may have fundamentally changed our own relation to speech. On the whole, however, he wants to avoid genetic and psychological questions.

Given this desire to avoid psychologism, however, Ricoeur's argument against dialogue cited above does not necessarily follow. The idea of a dialogue with the text need not entail a dialogue with the author. Language speaks for itself whether it is spoken or written, Ricoeur's argument holds. Therefore he need not implicate the author. It is possible to have a dialogue with a text alone, without constructing a person behind the text. Since Ricoeur admits that it is good procedure to treat the author as if he were dead when dealing with the text ("QT" 183, see also 185), he should also admit that the text can respond to questions if the inquirer looks for the answers. In that sense a text is perhaps a better partner in dialogue than its author, since it always says what it means and never changes its "mind."

Along with the important difference between the referential function of speech and that of the text, Ricoeur recognizes that the utterance also involves a context which surrounds it and guarantees the possibility of reference. The text, he argues, represents not only an interruption of the dialogue but, simultaneously, an interception of the reference. Whereas in speech to refer is often to show or to demonstrate, in poetic writing the context or situation is absent, as is the possibility of direct ostensive reference. Ricoeur, however, suggests that the reference of a text is only interrupted and never completely suppressed. He resists what he calls "the ideology of the absolute text" whereby the text is said to be autonomous and context-free.

The text, we will see, is not without reference; it will be precisely the task of the reading qua interpretation to effectuate the reference. At least, in this suspense where the reference is deferred, the text is in some sense "in the air," outside the world or without world. By means of this obliteration of the connection to the world each text is free to enter into relation with all other texts that come to take the place of the circumstantial reality shown by living speech.

This relation of text to text, in the effacement of the world about which one speaks, engenders the quasi-world of texts, or *literature*.   ["QT" 184]

While this suggestion that the reference of texts to other texts creates a body of literature is valuable, it does not do complete justice to the phenomenon of *poetic* literature. Ricoeur's description fits "literature" in one sense of the term—the "literature" on a subject matter or particular field (for example, the philological literature on Goethe). But there is a difference between texts that are more closely situated, secondary, and circumstantial and texts that are poetic and primary. Because of this *prima facie* difference, a distinction is often made between ordinary texts and immanent texts,[8] between those texts with a more clearly defined context and those that seem to be context-free, "hors monde ou sans monde." These latter texts can be said to be outside the world and without external reference insofar as they are self-referential and create their own world. The reference of such texts cannot be reduced merely to their relation to other texts, since such a reduction denies their essential uniqueness and individuality.

In a later paper Ricoeur himself qualifies his injunction against "absolute" or immanent texts by admitting the existence of at least a few such texts: "Only a few sophisticated texts satisfy this ideal of a text without reference."[9] Since he still holds that all texts must be about something but since there is no ostensive reference in these privileged texts, Ricoeur suggests that the reference of these texts is not to something *in* the world but to the world as such. Or, to use Heideggerian language, the reference is not to the world, but to the worldhood of the world.[10] In another article concerned more directly with literary texts per se, Ricoeur adds that the literary text creates a "possible world."[11] This suggestion demonstrates that he is not in fact opposed to the idea of immanence in poetic texts, since he allows here for the text's creation of its own world rather than restricting the scope of the reference of the literary text to the world of everyday reality and preestablished, ordinary meanings. Ricoeur too, then, wishes to say that "a work does not only mirror its time, but it opens up a world which it bears within itself." He recognizes, furthermore, that our access to immanent, or uniquely individual, texts is only perspectival. He even speaks of the "intention of the text" itself, thus vitiating some of his concern about the inappropriateness of the term "dialogue."[12]

Ricoeur's apparent objections to the dialogical model are not, therefore, serious criticisms of Gadamer's theory. In fact, Ricoeur's theory follows Gadamer's in depsychologizing the hermeneutics of Dilthey (see "QT" 200). Further, Ricoeur is struggling to reduce the arbitrariness of the hermeneutic concept of appropriation employed by Schleiermacher, Dilthey, and Bultmann. The concept of appropriation as found in these thinkers generally entails the notion that the meaning of the text is what the interpreter finds to be relevant to his own sphere of interest. By arguing that explication and interpretation are not antithetic poles of a bifurcation but are necessarily intertwined, Ricoeur hopes to show that appropriation need not be arbitrary.

His goal at least in the essay "Qu'est-ce qu'un Texte?" is to develop what can be called a structuralist hermeneutics. This theory is intended to guarantee that interpretation will be objective and that appropriation, although necessary, will not be arbitrary; that is to say, it will not represent the subjective imposition of the interpreter's context on the text. His structuralist hermeneutics is thus based on the integration of formalist explication and meaningful interpretation. "If, then, the intention is the intention of the text, and if this intention is the direction that it opens for thought, it is necessary to understand the deep semantics in a fundamentally dynamic sense; I will hence say this: to explicate is to free [dégager] the structure, that is to say, the internal relations of dependence which constitute the static of the text; to interpret is to set out on the path of thought opened by the text, to start out on the way to the *orient* of the text" ("QT" 198).

Will this theory account for the interpretation of poetic texts as well as ordinary ones? The distinction between ordinary and immanent texts appears to be essential in order to do justice to the phenomenon of artistic literature and to separate this sense of the word "literature" from the sense of the "literature" on a particular subject or field. Precisely this poetic immanency, however, creates a problem for the literature (in the second sense) that must explicate and interpret the immanent text. How can the poetic text determine or guarantee the validity or appropriateness of the interpretive context when the text itself transcends any interpretive attempt to connect its immanence with external reference? Such immanence makes any appropriation seem arbitrary. Any hermeneutics must take a stand on the problem of the relation of the interpretive context to the poetic text.

III. APPROPRIATION

The traditional sense of appropriation sees it as a separate act wherein the text is made "relevant" to the present interests of the interpreter. It is not the sense Gadamer intends when he speaks of the moment of application. *Anwendung* (application) is not to be confused with *Aneignung* (appropriation). The danger of the notion of appropriation as it is traditionally conceived (and of the notion of "relevance" as used today) lies in its implication of psychologism and subjectivism, in its suggestion that the interpretation is determined more by the whims of the interpreter than by the nature of the text.

Ricoeur's structuralist hermeneutics seeks to avoid psychologism and arbitrariness by making the appropriation dependent on a scientific, structuralist, strictly intrinsic explication of the text. But apparently the effort has forced Ricoeur into a dogmatic belief in method, into the illusion of an objective *beginning* for interpretation. His attempt to reconcile the method of structuralism with philosophical hermeneutics conflicts with the spirit of Heidegger's and Gadamer's ontological hermeneutics, producing difficulties for Ricoeur, who also, after all, sees the hermeneutic circle as an ontological, and not a psychological, principle.

Ricoeur does understand the principle of appropriation in rather traditional terms. He sees it as involving a struggle with cultural and historical distance and an overcoming of this distance through the "relevancy" of the interpretation for the present ("le caractère 'actuel' de l'interprétation"—"QT" 195). Ricoeur thinks that this "actualization" of the text's meaning will "retake its intercepted and suspended movement of reference toward a world and its subjects" ("QT" 195). Appropriation is, for him, the goal of interpretation, the end of the hermeneutical arch, "the anchoring of the arch in the ground of the lived" ("QT" 200).

This metaphor of the arch is, however, problematical. To say, as Ricoeur does, that the arch has its beginning in an objective explication and its end in an interpretive appropriation (an appropriation that is objective because of the validity of the starting point) is still to suggest a traditional *linear* account of understanding. A similar account is also defended by Hirsch, of whom Ricoeur speaks approvingly and uncritically. Linearity, however, conflicts with the fundamental principle of the hermeneutic circle; understanding is circular and not linear, since understanding is necessarily situated, and as the situation changes, so does the understanding (a change in understanding bringing about a change in the situation).

Ricoeur's arch metaphor tries to combine both objective linearity and hermeneutic circularity. But the notion of the beginning (Anfang) of interpretation by way of structuralist explication has not been made clear enough. Such a strictly intrinsic beginning would be impossible according to basic hermeneutic principles. Further, Ricoeur's concept of appropriation (as the goal of interpretation) appears too traditional. In the essay under discussion ("Qu'est-ce qu'un Texte?") he does retain the traditional sense of appropriation as "making familiar [propre] what was strange" ("QT" 195) and as being a separate act at the end of the process of explication and interpretation. While he maintains that psychological connotations are to be eliminated and tries to tie appropriation to a more objective starting point, perhaps he should have gone further and offered a more fundamental criticism of the ideas of method and appropriation.

These questions must be considered in detail. First, we must be aware that the problem of the beginning goes back to a criticism Hegel makes of the sciences. His smaller *Logic* argues that all the sciences—except philosophy, which is circular—are based on some form of subjective presupposition and hence cannot, qua science, justify their beginnings.[13] This argument applies as well to literary study which claims to be scientific (structural), and especially to Roland Barthes's "science of literature,"[14] which makes literature into an object ("un object écrit"—*CV* 56) and claims to be, like linguistics, a "science of the content's *conditions,* i.e., of the forms" (*CV* 57). Ricoeur does argue that such a purely syntactic kind of explication, whether of linguistic structures or of myth structures (for example, those from Lévi-Strauss), would be sterile if it did not also raise the semantic problems underlying it as a "recovery of meaning" ("reprise du sens"—"QT" 197). If Ricoeur is right, it follows that the unveiling of the structures is conditioned by a context of interest exterior to the literary work. This context has its beginnings not in the text itself but in the motivation of the scientist-interpreter. Ricoeur's argument also implies that the idea of *one* science of literature is a mistake, since there can be as many valid interpretational approaches as there are social or humanistic sciences (Geisteswissenschaften). The text demonstrates its ability to be brought into any number of coherent contexts, at the same time transcending any single context.

Hence the results of structuralist explication may very well be interesting and contribute to the reading of texts, but the implicit claim that such results are scientific can be misleading. A science presupposes its beginnings insofar as it has chosen the model and scope of the reality of which it proceeds to investigate *instances*. The structuralist investigation sees different texts as different instances of a broader, more universal reality. But an immanent text creates its own context or, more precisely, has no context other than itself. Since it does not depend on external reference to be meaningful, it demands that the explication be primarily oriented to it alone, even if such a demand is impossible to meet.

Structuralist "science" can reply (as Ricoeur does)[15] that it begins by looking only at features of the text itself and thus is purely intrinsic. This argument assumes, however, that a kind of pure observation, free of theory, exists. But science itself provides evidence that seeing is always "seeing as"—that is, perception is always *context-determined*. Furthermore, scientific seeing is "seeing that" (for example, seeing that such and such will occur), whereby the perception occurs within a conceptual framework and entails an understanding of the conditions and consequences of the operant system of meanings. Thus, perception is also *theory-determined*. A structuralist who finds "mythèmes" (syntactic elements of myth structures) should therefore not be so naïve as to assume that the text itself reveals these to him and that his own theory has not influenced his findings.

Sciences are themselves kinds of interpretations. For the natural sciences this is not a problem, since there is general agreement as to what constitutes the object of investigation. But literary investigation, contrary to Ricoeur's image, is not an arch but a circle: it cannot take its beginnings for granted, since these are precisely what it is trying to investigate. The reality of the text is not a given; it is what the explication tries to decipher. Even this idea of explication as a deciphering of reality is misleading, however, for poetry is not completely analogous to nature. Thus, Hölderlin's view of poetry suggests that poetic meaning resists and transcends efforts to lay bare some underlying reality, some one definite, univocal meaning.

Does hermeneutic theory of interpretation itself have a problem of *Anfang?* Gadamer believes that it does not, and the reason for this is linked to the second problem accompanying Ricoeur's structuralist hermeneutics—the problem of appropriation. A theory of interpretation with psychologistic presuppositions assumes that, since the text was the creation of another individual consciousness and the interpreter himself is an individual consciousness, a common sphere of interest, a shared context of experience, underly the historical or cultural differences. Suspicions about these assumptions lead to the turn to formalism and, at an extreme, to the hope for a logic or even a science of interpretation as a way to prevent arbitrariness. But this scientism is still a kind of appropriation, which assumes that a common underlying reality joins the world of the text with the world of the interpreter. The arbitrariness of scientistic appropriation begins to manifest itself in the pluralism of "approaches" to the text and of structures. In trying to avoid relativism, a new kind of relativism emerges. This is evident in Lévi-Strauss's view that structures are myths and that a wide range of structural analysis, from the microlevel of almost imperceptible elements to the macrolevel of generalizations about the human condition, must be allowed and even admitted to be of equal validity.

The scientistic retreat to a belief in the complete objectivity of method can lead only to a mistaken view of the nature of understanding and interpretation. This crucial point is again suggested by the ironic title of Gadamer's book, *Truth and Method.* The irony is intentional, since the hermeneutic insight claims that truth cannot be guaranteed by method. Understanding is not a matter of acquiring eternally true knowledge about a previously given real-ity. On the contrary, it is itself a concrete happening, a form of doing and creating that has consequences (Wirkungen) in and of itself. Gadamer's original plan to call his book *Verstehen und Geschehen* (perhaps best translated as "Understanding and Hap-pening," although *Geschehen* is difficult to translate because it is also a technical term in Heidegger's later philosophy) suggests more positively the force and direction of his philosophical her-meneutics.

Specifically in regard to the theory of art, Gadamer argues that the encounter with art is not a matter of aesthetic disinterested-ness. Rather, it is an "Ineinanderspiel von Geschehen und Ver-stehen," an interplay of happening and understanding (*WM* 520). Gadamer's argument that *Verstehen* and *Geschehen* are so closely connected is intended precisely to undercut and show the limita-tions of the modern technological-scientific outlook with its belief in the truth of completely objective method. The scientific assump-tion of the possibility of neutral, objective observation and a neu-tral starting point overlooks the fact that the scientific viewpoint is only one possible attitude and that there may be a fundamental in-compatibility between a context involving the technicoscientific outlook and one that does not. The hermeneutic argument implies that literary studies are most fundamentally not "scientific" and linear in nature but *historical* and circular (in a nonvicious sense). They are historical not merely in that they are concered with the past, but also in that they address the historical consequences of the encounter with the art work. The circularity occurs in the con-stant necessity to rethink the reception of the art work because of changes in their own historical situation.

A fundamental mistake of a linear objectivism is to forget this historicity and to assume that the meaning of the text is a given, an in-itself, which only needs to be unfolded. "Hermeneutics," Gad-amer holds, "has to see through the dogmatism of a 'meaning-in-itself' just as much as the critical philosophy had to see through the dogmatism of experience" (*WM* 448). Hermeneutical theory itself is not such a dogmatism:

Totally different is the case of hermeneutic awareness [wirkungsgeschichtliches Bewusstsein] in which the hermeneutic experience is completed. It knows of the

interminable openness of the occurrence of meaning [Sinngeschehen] in which it
participates. . . . There is no possible consciousness—we have repeatedly emphasized this, and the historicity of understanding depends on this—there is no possible consciousness, even if it were an infinite one, in which the content [die
"Sache"] that is passed down shines in the light of eternity. Each appropriation
[Aneignung] of the tradition is a historically different one—which does not mean
that each would be only a dim recording of the same: each is on the contrary the
experience of a viewpoint on the subject matter [Sache] itself.   [*WM* 448]

In that sense, no one appropriation can claim to be the only
objective and correct one; it can only be useful for a particular
time and purpose. The mistake behind the traditional notion of
appropriation is to assume that the appropriation evolves directly
out of a foregoing, intrinsic explication and that the particular
application involved in the appropriation of the explication (in the
conscious attempt to determine the relevance of the explication to
present interests) does not alter the objectivity of the intrinsic explication. Gadamer's argument recognizes that the *applicatio*
(Anwendung) involved in the process of interpretation is not
merely a later, explicit effort; it is already implicitly operant in the
very beginnings of the encounter with the literary text and the historical past.

The contingency of historical, hermeneutic understanding thus
makes such understanding different from scientific appropriation:
historical understanding must constantly challenge its own activity
and assumptions. More important, Gadamer's analysis reveals
how the hermeneutic understanding demands a self-understanding. In order to understand the past, it is necessary to try to understand one's own presuppositions and prejudgments in order to
realize how these mediate one's perception of the past. At the
same time, since the present can only be understood by acquiring
some distance from it, the inquiry into the past is an essential step
in coming to an understanding of the present and of its inherence
in a tradition. The beginnings of hermeneutical thinking are not
problematical in the same way that the beginnings of a science are.
These onsets are not left unquestioned and unexamined; they must
be continually rethought. Only the objectivist theory of interpretation, with its belief in the absoluteness of its beginning, in the complete objectivity of its method, would encounter such a difficulty.

Of course Gadamer's insistence that each appropriation is conditioned by and relative to its historical setting does not answer all

the questions raised by the problem of appropriation, even granted that his account exposes a false methodological self-understanding of the relation of explication and appropriation. Some questions remain. Can an immanent text be placed into any interpretive context whatsoever? What are the boundaries of context? Is a context ever too wide or too narrow? How binding on the interpretation is the text's own historical context? What is the relation between literary interpretation and literary history? While Gadamer may never be able to answer these questions to the full satisfaction of an objectivist, he can give arguments that do justice to most people's intuitions about the historicity of interpretation.

IV. THE HISTORICITY OF INTERPRETATION

The framework of Gadamer's position on the questions of immanence, historicity, and context can be summarized concisely. He does not hesitate to state that the context of the interpretation of the immanent text is the interpreter's context. This does not mean that the interpretation is arbitrary or subjective, since the interpreter's own context is itself conditioned by the tradition in which he stands, and the text is part of this tradition. Without paradox it can thus be said that the immanent text is both context-free and context-bound. It is context-free in the sense that the text is its own reference, and context-bound in that the text appears to its readers in a horizon of interest, in a context implicitly brought to the text by the reader. Such a context can be revised in terms of the text, but will always be only partial because of the basic asymmetry between the immanence of the text's language and the necessary historicity of the emergence of the meaning of that language in interpretive understanding.

This summary and elaboration of Gadamer's position takes into account a number of different elements in his hermeneutic theory, but two concepts must be stressed to show why historical understanding is neither subjective nor impossible. These are Gadamer's concepts of *Horizontverschmelzung* and *wirkungsgeschichtliches Bewusstsein.* The former is intended to explain the possibility of historical understanding, while the latter becomes a guiding ideal of proper interpretation.

The notion of *Horizontverschmelzung,* or fusion of horizons, is

Gadamer's alternative to a psychologistic account of historical understanding. The term "horizon" is an attempt at describing the situatedness or context-bound character of interpretation. Unlike the literalist or objectivist, who believes that his observation is neutral, Gadamer argues that one person's perception of another situation is always laden with previous understanding of his own situation. The interpreter is not, however, limited exclusively to the context or situation he had before approaching the text. Gadamer is aware that Friedrich Schlegel's ironic account of the logic of typical historical criticism includes an axiom of the "customary"; in Schlegel's words: "Axiom of the Customary: The way it is with us and around us is the way it must have been everywhere, since all of that is so natural!"[16] A horizon, Gadamer argues, is not closed; rather, it is flexible and open—it moves with us as we move within it (*WM* 288).

Furthermore, the horizon is precisely what allows for distinctions between the near and the far, the large and the small (*WM* 286). The objectivist is also forced to make these discriminations —for instance, in his selection of what counts as evidence or in his decision about what is important and what is not. He only deludes himself when he thinks that his own horizon or context is not influencing his account. It is impossible to separate oneself (Von-sich-absehen) completely from one's own horizon. On the other hand, the past moment in which one is interested must also have been enclosed in a horizon. Does it follow, then, that it is impossible ever to understand that horizon? Here there is no suggestion, as in some versions of historicism, that the past is unknowable. Although Gadamer denies that the past is knowable *in itself* (in a strict sense of "knowable"), apart from any mediation or contamination by the present, an understanding of the horizon of the past does become possible with the idea of a horizon as flexible and open.

The horizon of the interpreter can be expanded to include the horizon of the past. (This fusion of horizons should not be confused, however, with appropriating the past completely into one's own stance nor with knowing the past as it was for itself.) The fusion results in a new horizon. On the one hand, fusion involves a broadening of the present horizon—as historical study is often said to dispel certain prejudices and induce tolerance. On the other, it also involves a focusing of the past horizon in such a way that things which may have been mere adumbrations become definite factors in that horizon—perhaps because of subsequent occurrences—while other factors disappear—perhaps because certain events failed to take place. Gadamer argues that understanding the past is analogous to understanding another person (as a Thou) insofar as placing oneself in the other's place (Sichversetzen) is never disregarding oneself (Von-sich-absehen). To recognize the other's irreducible individuality, one has to respect him as one would respect oneself. The *Sichversetzen* involves a *sich-selber-mit-bringen*, a bringing of oneself into the situation (*WM* 288). Furthermore, merely putting oneself in the other's place would not bring about the desired understanding of the problem at hand—that is, of the subject matter (Sache).

Within the enlarged horizon, however, there can be an awareness of the differences among previous horizons. There can also be a realization that the understanding of the past is conditioned by the present. Thus, although someone may think he has gained a good understanding of the past as it appeared to itself, he must realize that his understanding is still conditioned by the present—still itself historically conditioned. Therefore the interpretation is necessarily incomplete, since further questions about one's own situation have to be answered in order to know how these influenced one's questioning of the past. Further, the interpretation is itself provisional—that is, conditioned by its own historical setting and by certain interests. This setting and these interests are themselves going to be modified and changed. This double awareness is what Gadamer calls *wirkungsgeschichtliches Bewusstsein*.[17] The concept has critical force, since it indicates the nature of *proper* interpretation: "A truly historical thinking must also think its own historicity" (*WM* 283).

Gadamer himself raises the question that naturally comes to mind: why talk about a fusion of horizons and not just a building of one horizon? The term "fusion" (Verschmelzung) is indeed misunderstood if it is believed, as some accounts of Gadamer seem to indicate, that the fusion is a *reconciliation* of the horizons, a flattening out of the historical and perspectival differences. Although Gadamer does claim that a *single* horizon results (*WM* 288), it must be remembered that a horizon is in flux and that the hermeneutic consciousness maintains a *tension* between the historical consciousness (of the past) and the strictly present horizon (Gegenwartshorizont). Without such tension, understanding of the past as different from the present would indeed be impossible; it is precisely the tension that allows us to become aware of our preunderstandings as our own.

This discussion of historical understanding extends itself quite naturally to textual understanding, especially since most texts (and in a certain sense all texts) belong to a past, even if a recent past. A plausible case can even be made for claiming that no text is ever contemporary. Such a statement would have little heuristic value, however, since it makes the scope of the present too narrow for any practical purpose. The past, however, is often available to us only in the form of a text, and even the recent past is accessible only in a report involving a selection of evidence based on a decision as to what is important. Thus, the past is, in a certain sense, a "story."

There is, then, a very concrete difference between this historical horizon and the present horizon in the hermeneutic consciousness, for the former is written while the latter is not yet written. Gadamer has argued[18] that writing is essential to all art, since writing involves a total congruence of intention and the intended, a total adequacy of meaning. While all art is not necessarily reducible to writing, art aspires to the ideal which writing manifests, this ideal being "to be what it means." Literary writing has a priority because it represents the most extreme and, for Gadamer, the paradigmatic form of writing. According to Gadamer, literary writing is the strangest, yet the most interpretation-demanding form of writing. In its interpretation the claim of the past on the present is most fully experienced (*WM* 156). Hence the interpretation of literary texts becomes paradigmatic for the interpretation of other texts, *including* historical texts.

It is writing that preserves the connection of the past with the present in a tradition. The text is not simply a piece of the past but continues to have meaning whenever it is read. The historical gap between present and past is bridged by the relation of interpreter and text, and this relation is a phenomenon of *language,* of linguisticality (Sprachlichkeit). For Gadamer the phenomenon investigated by hermeneutic questioning—whether the subject matter be literary, historical, juridical, or whatever—is language itself.

On this point Gadamer's analysis of language comes very close to Heidegger's. Language is historical, but in such a way as to be the source of the historical. A particular language is tied to a particular historical setting. "Language" here means the way the situation is encountered, the way problems are phrased, and the way the future is anticipated. But this language is discovered in a text or set of texts by an interpreter who speaks a different language. The historical difference can thus be seen as a difference between languages. But what about the language that mediates these differences? Clearly it is only through language that the differences can even be compared. Thus language is a major factor in the very continuity of the tradition connecting past and present. Yet the language does not overcome the differences; it does not completely bridge the gap, for as it brings certain features of each world or horizon to light, it conceals other features. Similarly, the text itself must have functioned in the same way, clarifying certain features of the actual situation that were perhaps only dim adumbrations before, at the same time concealing other features. Language is essentially entrenched in history, then, insofar as it is limited to particulars and can never reveal the whole as such. At the same time language is the essence of history, for it is this process of revealing and concealing that demands further accounts and further actions. Accounts and actions are linked, for an action is taken according to the account that is believed, while accounts are themselves actions, since they structure the situation and sometimes alter it.

Because of the insistence on the essential interconnections between the concepts of linguisticality and historicity, hermeneutic theory can reconcile the apparent conflict at issue in this chapter between the immanence of the poetic text and the historicity of interpretation. There is no contradiction in asserting both that some texts need to be treated as if they were completely immanent and that those texts can appear to us only in the partial perspective of inadequate interpretations. *Both* poetry and interpretation are essentially historical in nature. Once written, the language of the text is freed from the constraints under which it may originally have been conceived. Any action can have consequences that exceed the expectations of the agent, and these consequences may give rise to the necessity for other actions which the agent did not anticipate. True of the poetic text, this is equally true of the interpretive text. The interpretation may appear to have thrown new light on the poetic text, but as time goes by, other aspects of the poetry may gradually appear to have been eclipsed either by the very brightness of the interpretive illumination or by the shadows caused by the angle of incidence. Thus, immanence of the poetic text turns out to be another name for the historicity of interpretation. That a poetic text appears to transcend particular interpretive understandings leads us to call it immanent. Yet it would be a mistake to believe that this immanence implies a transcendence *beyond* history or *outside* history—into the eternal, for instance. Rather, because the transcendence is tied to the history of a dialogue with the poem, it is always further *into* history, into another context of interpretation.

The hermeneutic position holds, then, that interpretation is not merely a possible way of relating to the poem, but that it is the necessary way. To be understood at all, the poem must be engaged in a dialogue that creates a context or meaning—it must be interpreted. Interpretation is inevitable.

FOUR
Truth and Criticism

Hölderlin's idea that poetry sees with a new innocence—"alles ist wie zum erstenmale"—gives poetic language a primacy over the more encumbered ordinary ways of speaking. Furthermore, poetry is not merely a mode of fiction. Rather, poetry results from the poet's contact with the gods and his mediation between them and ordinary men. As the fragment beginning "Wie wenn am Feiertage" indicates, however, the poetic task is not without danger, for the poet stands unprotected before a vision which may preclude his returning to the world and sharing in the peace brought about by his sacrifice of himself through his song:

> Doch uns gebührt es, unter Gottes Gewittern,
> Ihr Dichter! mit entblösstem Haupte zu stehen,
> Des Vaters Strahl, ihn selbst, mit eigner Hand
> Zu fassen und dem Volk ins Lied
> Gehüllt die himmlische Gabe zu reichen.[1]

To say that poetry is a "himmlische Gabe," a "heavenly gift," is to imply that it is both forceful and true.

What is the nature of this truth? Schopenhauer suggests that the truth of art is transhistorical in the sense of being eternal, "himmlisch" in the sense of being a suspension of the worldly will. Heidegger holds that truth is radically historical, and Gadamer also argues that aesthetic consciousness is grounded in and made possible by the hermeneutic-historical consciousness (see *WM* 157). The hermeneutic position, however, appears to surrender to the aesthetic position the basis for the truth of art and the truth of interpretations of art works. To give up truth is to give up criticism —both the criticism of one interpretation by another and that implicit in the contrast between the ideal world of the art work and the real world, past and present. The alternative to the danger of the "heavenly gift" appears to be the equally dangerous nihilistic abyss of historicist relativism.

A central difficulty in explaining hermeneutical theory comes from the necessity of distinguishing it both from metaphysical idealism and from a discussion of particular literary critical methods or strategies. A discussion of *method* involves discussion of how to read a book or debate about the merits of different "approaches." A discussion of *methodology,* on the other hand, must be more abstract and philosophical; it belongs at the level of the theory of knowledge and of understanding. These two levels of discussion are not easily kept distinct, since they are closely related. According to the hermeneutical notion of understanding, some approach to a text, some interpretive context, is always necessary; access to a text is always perspectival and partial, mediated by preunderstandings and biases or prejudgments (Vorurteile). The question is whether this methodological claim rules out critical discussion both of the conditions for interpretive understanding and of the criteria for these interpretations, though the criteria make possible the distinction between more adequate and less adequate approaches.

Critics of Gadamer's position focus precisely on the possibility of such conditions and criteria. They see in Gadamer's hermeneutics the danger of historical relativism. To test Gadamer's position against these critics, several questions must be raised and clarified. Does it follow from Gadamer's argument (that the poetic text must be brought into an interpretive context determined by the possibilities implicit in a particular historical-cultural setting) that the meaning of the poetic text is indeterminate?[2] Does such an argument preclude contesting alternative "approaches" to a text or conflicting "contexts" of interpretation? Is the hermeneutic-historical situation constitutive of the interpretation in such a way that criticism of both the interpretation and the ideology of that situation is impossible? These are questions of methodology, and while the answers to such questions will not supply a new method or approach to texts, they have practical consequences for understanding what is involved in interpretation.

Whereas the central question of the previous chapter was the possibility of *interpretation,* this chapter will concern itself with the possibility of *criticism.* The question of criticism has been raised not only in the more limited concern with the possibility of criticism of text interpretations (E. Betti), but also, more broadly, with the possibility of criticism of the tradition as such, of ideologies (J. Habermas). We will review a number of such objections to Gadamer's theory in order to determine the extent to which this philosophical question about criticism can be answered. And if a case can be made that according to the tenets of hermeneutic theory criticism is possible, then on hermeneutic grounds it is also justifiable to speak of the *truth* of the interpretation—that is, of its validity and legitimacy.

I. THE HISTORICITY OF ART

In opposition to Gadamer's hermeneutics, Oskar Becker claims correctly that hermeneutics presupposes a fundamental belief in historicity as the authentic being of man. He argues that for those opposed to this belief, the hermeneutic arguments are less effective. Schopenhauer, for instance, would not be persuaded. Furthermore, Becker sees no grounds for dispute over this difference between the aesthetic attitude and the historical-hermeneutic attitude, since debate finally depends upon "what kind of man one is."[3] But insofar as these attitudes have different consequences, the desirability of one over the other can certainly be debated. In opposition to the hermeneutic thesis that the meaning of art is conditioned by its history of reception and influence (Wirkungsgeschichte), Becker prefers a more traditional aesthetic attitude, one derived from Kant's views about aesthetic distance and Schopenhauer's belief in the eternal, suprahistorical character of art works. He offers the following counterexample to the hermeneutic principles of the historicity of art:

One looks at a painting, but does not read it. An ancient vase painting or a statue is not an ancient text. We know some old cultures such as, for instance, Cretan or

Indus cultures only from their illustrated works that are "seeable" but not "readable" because the accompanying inscriptions are undeciphered so far. Can one not judge the artistic quality of these works merely because their humanistic-historical "content" cannot be interpreted?   [P. 230]

A similar counterexample, but from another field, comes from Franz Wieacker who insists on the historical autonomy of the legal test, just as Becker insists on the aesthetic autonomy of the art work. This insistence on autonomy implies the possibility and at times even the necessity of suspending the hermeneutic awareness of the history of effects and influence (wirkungsgeschichtliches Bewusstsein):

Then everywhere in the history of law there are findings and texts whose "history of effects" [Wirkungsgeschichte] has slumbered for thousands of years or begins at all only today with their discovery (as with accidentally discovered drafts, or with most contract documents, for example, of the Greco-Egyptian papyri, or, entirely, with completely buried or exotic legal cultures).[4]

Wieacker acknowledges the necessity of a certain preunderstanding in the form of a knowledge of the language and of relationships between other cultures. He contradicts Gadamer, however, by insisting both that there can be no continuity of tradition (Traditionszusammenhang) influencing or conditioning the researcher and that an "application" need not be involved in every understanding.

A similar objection is raised by Helmut Kuhn, who shares Wieacker's and Becker's concern that the capacity for true judgment is lost in the emphasis on historicity.

When man has a "historical essence" . . . , then his knowledge must also even in its principles be historically conditioned, or, as they say, "tied to a standpoint" [standpunktgebunden]. But does this then deserve the name of knowledge? Does it in fact happen that through the historiographical method we are deprived of truth?[5]

Kuhn holds that the European historian who wants to know the truth about, say, the history of Mongolia or of the Eskimo tribes can claim a completely disinterested, objective, aperspectival knowledge.

Gadamer himself replies to Kuhn, and this reply also applies to Wieacker's counterexample:

The history of North American Eskimo tribes is certainly completely independent from when and if these tribes worked into "European world history." And yet one can really not deny that the reflection on the history of effects [wirkungsgeschichtliche Reflexion] can show itself to be forceful even in terms of this historiographical task. Whoever reads the history of these tribes written today fifty or a hundred years from now will not only find this history out-of-date because of having learned more or having interpreted the sources more correctly in the meantime; he will also be able to attest that people in 1960 read the sources differently because they were moved by other questions, by other prejudices and interests.   [*WM* XVII-XVIII]

To claim that hermeneutical awareness is necessary simply because findings are likely to have shortcomings or questions are likely to become old-fashioned does not, however, completely rebut Wieacker's and Kuhn's objections. Furthermore, such a claim does not do justice to the concept of hermeneutic awareness itself, for it also involves a belief in and commitment to particular questions as crucial to their own age. In order to avoid making hermeneutics so potentially nihilistic, the objections must be countered in terms of larger issues.

It must first be emphasized that Gadamer's concept of hermeneutic awareness is not normative. It does not supply a *method* for understanding, nor does Gadamer claim this function for it. As his letter to E. Betti argues, his project is to analyze how understanding actually works, not how it should work: "*to acknowledge what is* rather than to start out from what one thinks should be the case or what one would like to be the case" (*WM* 484). Although Gadamer is not promoting any particular method, however, he is certainly promoting a *methodology* and contesting any methods based on unhistorical methodologies. Wieacker and Kuhn are mistaken to take Gadamer's principle of *wirkungsgeschichtliches Bewusstsein* as an implicit method rather than as a methodological principle. As a methodological principle it accounts for the very possibility of becoming aware of, and then suspending to a certain extent, one's own legal or cultural principles. Thus it makes possible the kind of knowledge that Wieacker and Kuhn fear will be lost.

This distinction between the levels of method and methodology leads to a second consideration that lends more support to Gadamer's reply. Is a statement of fact of the same logical order as a statement of a theory of historical contextualism? Is not the latter a second-order statement—that is, a statement about the former? The historicist is not necessarily disputing that there are facts; he is disputing certain claims made about those facts. Similarly, it cannot be objected that the historicist contradicts himself when he says that "everything is historical" on the grounds that this statement is believed by the historicist to be true eternally. Gadamer points out in his discussion of Leo Strauss (*WM* 504-505; see also *WM* 425) that the historicist statement does not necessarily entail paradox, and he adds the following hermeneutic note to the historicist thesis.

Then the thesis is indeed not that this sentence ["All knowledge is historically conditioned"] will always be taken to be true—just as it has not always been taken to be true. The historicism that takes itself seriously had better take into account that some day people will no longer accept this thesis as true and will think "unhistorically." [*WM* 505]

The effect of hermeneutics, then, is not to support the "moderns," who assert the primacy of the present over the past, in the classic dispute with the "ancients," who take the past as paradigmatic for the present. Rather, this whole dispute loses its force since hermeneutics investigates the very possibility of both viewpoints and the link between the viewpoints in the common project of self-understanding.

Scientific findings or historical facts per se are not under attack. What is rejected is an unhistorical methodology, the positing of a viewpoint outside history. On these grounds Becker's aesthetic attitude must be discarded. Becker's argument that we "see" rather than "read" an ancient painting, that a painting is not a text, may appear correct at first glance. Yet the aesthetic attitude also involves the idea that the work of art transcends any particular context, thus appearing *directly* to us as it is in itself, apart from our particular interests. As soon as we want to understand how the work of art (whether a poem or a painting) functions as art—that is, how and why it claims our attention—the hermeneutic task of understanding begins. Seeing the painting involves a project of investigation, both of the painting and of ourselves and our criteria and expectations for seeing the work as we do. Such a process of self-understanding must be in some sense a linguistic one, for it involves a process of question and answer leading to an articulated understanding. The painting is thus not so different from a text as it seems at first, especially if a text is not regarded as "dead" or "mute" language. The following passage in Gadamer's essay "Ästhetik und Hermeneutik" is an implicit reply to Becker:[6]

> The work of art says something to one, and not just in the manner that a historical document says something to the historian. It says something to each one as if it were said expressly to him, as something current and contemporary. So the task presents itself to understand the meaning of what is said and to make this understandable for oneself and others. Even the nonlinguistic work of art falls within the actual scope of the range of hermeneutic activities. It must be integrated into each one's self-understanding. [*KS* II 5]

According to Gadamer, then, there is no direct opposition between the aesthetic and the historical attitudes, as Becker holds. Rather, the aesthetic is a moment of the hermeneutic awareness, the moment that allows us to be claimed by the artwork as art. This aesthetic moment is complemented by the hermeneutic-historical task of achieving an understanding that is also a self-understanding. Gadamer's account makes art much more than a merely subjective phenomenon. It allows for the mediation of a historical tradition and a cultural setting. What an age considers art reveals a great deal about the age.

II. HERMENEUTICAL AND TRANSCENDENTAL TRUTH: KARL-OTTO APEL

Gadamer's rebuttal to the foregoing critiques is strengthened when a further point is clarified. The basic question underlying this discussion concerns the principle or criterion by which an interpretation can be said to be true. Gadamer's emphasis on the finitude and situatedness of the interpretive understanding makes it difficult to see how a claim to truth or even to validity can be made. One concept in Gadamer's analysis which appears to function as such a criterion is the "Vorgriff der Vollkommenheit" (the anticipation of perfection; see *WM* 278 f.)—the presupposition that the work embodies a unity of meaning (Einheit von Sinn), of a perfection of the kind attributed to an immanent text. According to Gadamer, this concept allows not only for the immanence of the text but also for its truth—that is, for the transcendence of the text's meaning toward the subject matter: "There is presupposed not only an immanent unity of meaning that gives the reader direction, but also a transcendental expectation of meaning that comes from the relation to the truth of what is meant and that also constantly guides the reader's comprehension" (*WM* 278).

Emilio Betti takes issue with Gadamer on this point, arguing that it is a delusion to think that the principle of *Vollkommenheit* accounts for the correctness (Richtigkeit) of understanding.[7] Like Wieacker and Kuhn, Betti believes that Gadamer's account of the historicity of the historian or interpreter shows that the historian must suspend all his own interests in order to have a disinterested knowledge of the intention of the original text. The expectations of the interpreter, according to Betti (see *HMG* 44 n. 95), should play no role until objective explication has taken place. But Betti, too, seems to have misunderstood Gadamer's concept of *wirkungsgeschichtliches Bewusstsein* as implying a method rather than a methodology. Furthermore, as Gadamer's decisive rebuttal (see *WM* 482 f.) shows, Betti is still caught in the psychologism of presupposing that the author's intention constitutes the basic meaning of the work and that understanding a text is the encounter of one mind with another.

More recently Karl-Otto Apel follows a line of criticism similar to Betti's but grounded in an account of hermeneutics which takes theory of language more seriously.[8] Apel proposes to rescue hermeneutics from relativistic historicism by suggesting that the former can recognize the historicity of interpretation even while positing a regulative concept of truth in the form of an ideal community of investigators (along the lines of Josiah Royce): "The sought-after regulative principle, in my opinion, lies in *the idea of the realization of an unlimited community of interpretation which everyone who argues* (and therefore, everyone who thinks!) *presupposes implicitly as an ideal instance of control*" (HD I 140). This concept of the community of investigators is modified according to an interpretation of Peirce and becomes a basic principle in the "transcendental hermeneutics" Apel is developing. The position sensibly holds that more than a mere subjective assertion of belief is needed to make an interpretation true, but then it must specify the intersubjective conditions for something to be true. Implicit in this theory of truth is the concept that *any rational being* would also think such and such to be true. The concept of truth thus undergoes a Kantian modification and becomes a *regulative* principle. Instead of being actually attained (or even attainable), truth is considered as necessarily, although only formally, implied in the act of asserting a judgment. Further, the principle takes into account the finitude of human reason and recognizes that all the conditions for making a judgment may not be specifiable or verifiable, and that some revisions may therefore turn out to be in order.

The advantage of a regulative principle of truth is that it allows for the possibility both of inadequate present knowledge and of criticism. Alternative interpretations and conflicting accounts can be criticized for such defects as obvious subjective bias. The point must also be stressed that a bias has to be discovered and proved; the mere metastatement that all accounts are biased does not itself carry any weight for this position. Finally, the regulative principle allows at least for the possibility of meaningfully asserting that an interpretation is true. "Truth" here means that the interpretation approximates the concensus of the ideal community of interpreters. On this theory truth is not the representation of a thing-in-itself but a function of social agreement.

Apel's position is similar to Gadamer's insofar as both emphasize the community or tradition of interests in which the investigator stands and to which he relates. On the other hand, Apel's position holds that the concept of an absolute truth is necessary as a regulative principle (*HD* I 140), and it adapts a Peircean concept by assuming that "in the long run" a final community of agreement can occur. This idea is potentially hermeneutical, however, rather than transcendental in a Kantian sense, because it emphasizes the historical progress of a community of investigators. Each step in the process of inquiry adds an irreversible element to the advancement of knowledge.

Gadamer's concept of the mediation of the tradition in our understanding of the past is in agreement with Apel's position insofar as both Apel and Gadamer insist that knowledge be grounded not in a subjective but rather in an intersubjective interaction. Gadamer's version of this idea is illustrated in his statement that the present understands the past, not *better* than the past understood itself, only *differently* (*WM* 280). Apel goes beyond Gadamer, however, when he sides with Peirce in thinking that it is necessary to posit a final consensus of the community of scientists in order to guarantee the objectivity of knowledge at an earlier stage:

> Peirce no longer presupposes, not even for natural science, a "consciousness in general" as the transcendental subject of objective truth; on the contrary, he, like the later K. Popper, grounds the possible objectivity of natural science in the historical process of understanding by the community of scientists. But he also starts from the principle that it is precisely this process of understanding, if it is not interrupted, that will produce *in the long run* the *consensus omnium* that the "transcendental consciousness in general" semiotically entails and that guarantees objectivity.   [*HD* I 132]

Insofar as both Gadamer and Apel make the possibility of truth contingent upon an intersubjective consensus rather than upon a transcendental subject, they are in agreement. Where they part ways is in Apel's positing an *ideal* consensus as a regulative principle. Like the concept of the "last historian," the concept of the "last scientist" who sees the "truth" of all previous stages of science is the projection of an unhistorical ideal that serves only to undercut the historical dimension of understanding with an unrealizable goal. To phrase the difference between Gadamer and Apel in another manner, both agree that knowledge is not subjective but is conditioned by the regulative principle of dependence on "what any rational being would also think." Gadamer's hermeneutic addition to this principle would be the stipulation "what any rational being *in that particular situation* would think." Thus Gadamer emphasizes the way the situation of the interpreter influences the perception of the text, or of the past, and why the interpretation can *legitimately* be believed to be true by the interpreter. (Here Hegel's *Phenomenology* supplies the model, and not, for instance, an empirical objectivism such as Ranke's.) In positing an unhistorical and theoretical final consensus, Apel is essentially agreeing with Betti (as Apel acknowledges to some extent; see *HD* I 141 n. 73) that understanding can occur only between minds of equal rank. Apel nevertheless adopts Gadamer's principle of *Vollkommenheit* (see *HD* I 142), apparently missing the point of the Betti-Gadamer debate.

The value of Gadamer's project lies in showing how differences in history, language, or culture can be made part of the process of understanding and can contribute to that process by allowing for an openness to further differences. Apel's view that an ideal community is necessary for truth overlooks the features of situational *phronesis* that Gadamer develops from Aristotle and sets forth for hermeneutics. In following Betti and thus making Gadamer into a subjectivist and existentialist, Apel does Gadamer an injustice. Apel himself expresses a preference for Peirce over Kant because of Peirce's emphasis on *praxis,* and precisely this preference brings Apel closer to Gadamer than might seem the case.

Gadamer replies to Apel on several of these points.[9] The central question as to how hermeneutics can be *Kritik* turns on the conception of the idea that understanding is always also *application.* It might be supposed that the idea of application means that the interpreter must apply his understanding *consciously* to a present situation, for example to make his knowledge "relevant" to present concerns. Or it can be assumed that it is unnecessary to apply one's knowledge in a "relevant" way while still acknowledging a demand that knowledge be *used* in some way, perhaps as criticism of other false understandings (as in Nietzsche's suggestion in the *Untimely Meditations* that history is to be used critically). While this latter point follows from Gadamer's notion, it is certainly not the central idea. Such a construal implies that the application of the understanding is indeed arbitrary and that in fact there is a distinction between the truth (or validity) of the understanding and the truth (or legitimacy) of the application. But Gadamer is concerned with different issues, for he argues that application is an "implicit moment of all understanding" ("R" 296). In other words, "application" takes on a new and distinct meaning within Gadamer's theory. Gadamer is making a philosophical point about the interest-bound character of all knowledge, and not a more normative point to the effect that all knowledge must be put to some use.

Although the statement about use may be true, under some construals it can be unhermeneutical. For instance, the argument that knowledge *should* be applied suggests that the subject is *free* to apply or not apply it. Such a conclusion runs counter to Gadamer's philosophical point that understanding as such is already application to a subject matter, a body of questions. Putting knowledge to use involves a conscious effort in addition to this more basic hermeneutical process of coming to an understanding. This explicit effort to be "relevant" involves on the one hand the attempt to become as aware as possible of unconscious preconceptions in order to be as objective ("disengaged") as is necessary, and on the other the attempt to reaffirm the value of the enterprise by seeing that the knowledge is used ("engaged").

"Application," then, has two distinct senses, depending on whether the discussion turns on a point of philosophical methodology or of actual method. The latter is sometimes called, as the discussion of Ricoeur indicated, "appropriation." The philosophical point, furthermore, has no normative force for the actual method of interpretation—it does not entail "engagement" or "relevance" as opposed to "disengagement" or "neutrality." Whether to emphasize "engagement" or "relevance" is less a theoretical question than a practical one, to be answered by the interpreter and judged by his readers.

The normative force of hermeneutical theory, Gadamer insists, comes only from the sense in which it "attempts to replace a bad philosophy with a better one" ("R" 297). The critical force of hermeneutical theory lies in its opposition to objectivistic philosophies of understanding, and it cuts against particular interpretations only if they can be shown to presuppose false attitudes about the nature of interpretation. Thus, the question "how is criticism possible" appears in a different light. A philosophical answer is not to be confused with dogmatic canon. Gadamer's hermeneutical concern is more essentially with what critics have to do (that is, with what is logically necessary) rather than with what they should do (that is, with what they can choose or fail to choose). Hermeneutical theory does not exclude praxis. On the contrary, the value of the theory is its explanation of the possibility of praxis. The analysis demonstrates that a sharp separation between theory and praxis is itself a false picture. It can be questioned whether the status of this hermeneutical assertion that theory and praxis are intertwined is theoretical or practical. Gadamer is aware of this ambiguity, and there will be occasion to return to it. For the present, however, it is important to understand more clearly the extent to which Gadamer accepts Apel's transcendental reading of hermeneutics.

In his "Replik" Gadamer admits that the transcendental force of hermeneutics is greater than would be the case if it were taken simply as implying a practical movement of making implicit, unconscious motives and assumptions explicit. He is willing to accept Apel's regulative idea of the infinite discourse of an unlimited community of interpretation ("R" 298, 313) only so long as this idea does not hide or imply a notion resembling Hegel's absolute knowledge. Gadamer argues that Hegel (in the *Phenomenology*) confuses completed knowledge with completed experience, when for the finite mind the completion of one form of experience leads only to an openness for new forms of experience ("R" 310-311; see *Kleine Schriften* III). Similarly, Gadamer attempts to modify Apel's suggestion that a transcendental community is presupposed in the judgment about the legitimacy of an interpretation. He dissociates the concept of *legitimation* from the Hegelian-Roycean concept of *progress* toward an ideal goal ("R" 299). While a dialectical contrast between interpretations may reveal an antithesis that leads to a new interpretation, Gadamer correctly sees no reason to hold that the new is a closer approximation to some final synthesis ("R" 299). Since the new is just as likely to cast new shadows as new light, there is no reason to expect that any interpretation will give more than aspects of the matter (Sache).

Gadamer's notion of the completeness or perfection (Vollkommenheit) of understanding remains *only* a regulative principle. He insists that in his phrase, *der Vorgriff der Vollkommenheit* (the anticipation of perfection), the accent on *"Vorgriff"* should not be overlooked, "since the superiority of that which is to be understood is never completely graspable in any interpretation" ("R" 302). The interpretation should, of course, attempt to assure its own legitimacy by striving to fulfill conditions that would lead to a consensus (although not necessarily a contemporary consensus, since one may reject the standards of colleagues and peers). To hold out such a consensus as an attainable goal, however, is to assume that meaning has a complete transparence—as Hegel, for instance, thought when he purported to decipher reason (a general plan with an end) in history.

The arguments against such an unhistorical understanding of meaning will be discussed more extensively (especially in relation to Pannenberg's concept of universal history). At this time an example of the practical force of Gadamer's resistance to the

Hegelian idealization of the transcendental-regulative principle is in order. Gadamer takes an example from his own field—classical philosophy—to indicate the various presuppositions held by different interpreters of Greek philosophers (such as Karl Reinhardt's concern with logical clarification and Werner Jaeger's with religious monotheism). Gadamer himself recognizes that his own interpretations are influenced by Heidegger's question of Being. These preconceptions or *Vorurteile* are not simply read into the Greeks; rather, there is a real attempt to understand these philosophers by seeing through and unmasking the *Vorurteile* of previous interpreters.

Interpretive *Vorurteile* can be productive, then, insofar as they bring to light the *previous* preconceptions or preunderstandings and correct them. The new interpretation makes this correction possible by the very contrast it represents to the old interpretation: the point where previous bias is recognized as such and unmasked, Gadamer points out, "will only be reached when what is right there in front of us is seen with new eyes" ("R" 298). Unless the scholar dealing with Aristotle attempts to see Aristotle in a new way, he will remain frozen in the perspectives and distortions of previous interpreters, perhaps even forgetting the possibility that there are distortions and becoming blind to criticism. Alternately, if the scholar senses the distortions, he may practice what Thomas Mann called "obscurantism"—attending to details in order to overlook the larger implications.

Hermeneutic theory thus does not make criticism impossible. On the contrary, hermeneutical reflection makes criticism necessary. The constant movement of interpretation requires awareness of the shadows cast on the texts by the old interpretations, and an attempt at illuminating these shadows by casting new light. Because interpretation is always partial, each interpretation, to the extent that it illuminates different portions of the subject matter, is at least implicitly a criticism of other interpretations. The real *practical* force, then, of hermeneutical reflection is this emphasis on the necessity of criticism. "In the long run" such an emphasis will be more forceful than any particular "approach," "school," or "method" of interpretation.

One difficulty with the foregoing account of criticism, however, is the negativity—some would say the emptiness—of the insistence on criticism. Gadamer's own example of the interpretation of Greek philosophers is, in fact, remarkably silent about what could be called the "appropriateness conditions" for interpretations, their context, and their *Vorurteile.* There is no discussion of whether some interpretive concepts are completely inappropriate. Gadamer's position is not indefensible, for it may very well be that establishing particular appropriateness conditions a priori is to revert to dogmatism. The only judge of the appropriateness of the context of one interpretation may be another interpretation, and perhaps "truth" in these matters *is* closely connected to (although it can never entirely be reduced to) "success"—that is, intersubjective agreement on the usefulness of the interpretations and their assumptions. In any case, a number of commentators have tried to argue that Gadamer does rely on implicit appropriateness conditions and that implicit concrete values are built into his program. These objections become especially urgent when the concern shifts from philology to social and historical understanding, which Gadamer includes as part of the universal scope of the hermeneutic theory of *Verstehen.* Because of the emphasis on the intersubjective community of interpretation, and specifically on the *tradition,* several writers have taken hermeneutics to be at least normative and at worst reactionary. These charges must be discussed to determine whether in fact appropriateness conditions should be specified more concretely if criticism is to be possible as well as necessary.

A positive feature of Apel's account is its extension of the vocabulary of hermeneutic theory to allow hermeneutic principles to be stated more clearly. The concept of tradition reinterpreted as a "community of interpretation and interaction" helps somewhat to offset a criticism made by Hirsch in his review of Gadamer. Hirsch argues that Gadamer holds "tradition" as a normative concept, implying that whoever follows the tradition is right and whoever does not is wrong (*VI* 250). Hirsch, like Betti, fails to realize that Gadamer is not offering a normative method. As Gadamer remarks in his "Replik" to Apel, hermeneutics does not "propagate a new praxis" ("R" 297). Hirsch's whole orientation differs from Gadamer's; he is more interested in knowing the norms that guarantee correct interpretation than in stating how understanding and interpretation are possible in the first place. Hirsch is misled into thinking that Gadamer's notion of historical understanding as a *Horizontverschmelzung* results in breaking down the two horizons of past and present into one that no longer can discern differences and tensions. Thus, he mistakenly argues that the fusion involves two distinct processes: the first, understanding the past text; and the second, applying this understanding to present concerns. This view confuses the two senses of "application." Nor does Gadamer claim that the second of these comes first, as Hirsch and Betti believe. Rather, he argues that the "first" process of understanding is itself mediated by the methodological presuppositions and the community of interests that constitute the tradition in which the interpreter stands. The tradition is not merely something with which to agree or disagree; rather, it is operant in every act of understanding.[10]

Hirsch and others are apparently misled by a false antinomy, one used by Nietzsche to produce paradox in his attack on objectivist historians. The antinomy depends on picturing the past as one closed circle and the present as another. The question of how one can get out of one circle or horizon into the other can never be adequately answered because the picture itself is abstract and false. Gadamer argues that the image is not derived from the nature of historical understanding itself, but rather from the positivistic ideal of objective, neutral procedure.

> To speak, as Nietzsche does, of historical consciousness as learning to place oneself in many changing horizons is not a correct description. *Whoever shuts his eyes to himself in that manner specifically does not have a historical horizon.* Nietzsche's demonstration of the disadvantage of history for life does not actually tell against historical consciousness as such, but rather against the self-alienation that occurs when historical consciousness takes the modern historical scientific method to be its genuine essence.   [*WM* 289; emphasis added]

The misunderstanding by many of Gadamer's readers of such concepts as tradition points to a deeper misinterpretation of the philosophical scope of Gadamer's theory, of its claim to be *philosophical* hermeneutics. In this regard Apel's transcendental additions to hermeneutical philosophy also serve to raise the debate beyond a concern with the methods of particular humanistic disciplines. The transcendental or *universal* character aspired to by hermeneutical philosophy means that it is not even restricted to the methodology of the *Geisteswissenschaften*. Recent work carries hermeneutics into the methodology of the social sciences and the natural sciences as well.

The philosophical issues behind Gadamer's claim to this universality have been hotly contested in the famous *Hermeneutikstreit*. Although many philosophers in Germany have participated in this discussion of Gadamer's work, the principal exchange takes place between Gadamer and Jürgen Habermas. The present-day status of hermeneutics cannot be understood without knowing about this debate, and thus the essentials will be reviewed here.

III. THE GADAMER-HABERMAS DEBATE

The original exchange between Habermas and Gadamer occurred in 1967. Habermas included a discussion of hermeneutics in his critical survey of recent work in sociology and social theory entitled *Zur Logik der Sozialwissenschaften*.[11] He sided with Gadamer insofar as the latter's hermeneutics represents a criticism of the unreflective character of positivistic theory of social science (*ZLS* 172). On the other hand, Habermas also suspected Gadamer's theory of a tendency toward relativism and of a lack of critical reflection on the ontological basis it derives from Heidegger.

Despite Gadamer's reply in "Rhetorik, Hermeneutik und Ideologiekritik,"[12] Habermas indirectly shows in his book *Erkenntnis und Interesse* (1968) that he still considers the hermeneutical description of the sciences relevant only to the sociohistorical disciplines.[13] The hermeneutical dimension is not universal and all-inclusive, but subordinate to the even more reflective level of Habermas's own concern with *Ideologiekritik*—social criticism of ideologies modeled on the paradigm of psychoanalysis. The question thus is whether hermeneutics is subject to ideology criticism or whether the latter is itself accounted for by the hermeneutical theory of understanding.

Habermas explicitly contests Gadamer's claim to the universality of hermeneutics in the essay he contributed to Gadamer's 1970 *Festschrift*,[14] and Gadamer's "Replik" in turn appeared in the 1971 anthology entitled *Hermeneutik und Ideologiekritik*.[15] Most recently Habermas has gone on to develop a theory of com-

munication and of truth that he calls "universal pragmatics."
Clearly claiming a universality for itself, this theory has close affinities with Apel's transcendental hermeneutics in drawing on
Apel's Peirce interpretation. Habermas does not discuss the relation of this theory to Gadamer's, but Gadamer has registered his
reservations in the new "Nachwort" to the third edition of *Wahrheit und Methode* (1975).

Although the details of this debate have changed as Habermas,
the younger man of the two, has developed and modified his own
philosophical program, the crucial issue has remained the same
throughout. Is it possible for philosophy itself to stay within the
hermeneutical circle of understanding, and within the limitations
imposed by its own historical conditions, yet legitimately posit
rational principles as conditions for the possible validity or truth
of particular acts of understanding? Habermas continues to hold
to a notion of reason demanding such transcendental principles,
and Gadamer still maintains that such faith in the power of reflection alone represents an idealization that falsely attempts to break
out of the hermeneutical circle.

Whereas Habermas's essays appearing since 1970 increasingly
focus on the theory of truth, the earlier essays question whether
Gadamer's claim that the tradition is constitutive of understanding needs to be supplemented by a theory of universal history in
order to escape a relativistic historicism. Thus, central to the
debate are the questions, can the tradition itself be criticized, and
can reflection emancipate itself from its historical conditions?
Theories such as Marxism certainly maintain that there are standards growing out of history that nevertheless can be used both to
criticize the status quo and to advance history toward the ultimate
goals posited by these standards. A theory of history need not be
so materialistic, however, and Habermas's criticism of Marx
shows that he is interested more in the epistemological aspects of
such a theory.[16]

In this regard Habermas goes so far as to ally Gadamer with
Nietzsche on the problem of standards for historical criticism and
Nietzsche's subjectivization of science:

Nietzsche's embarrassment is the same with regard to the cultural sciences as to
the natural sciences. He cannot abandon the claim of the positivist concept of

science, while being unable to cast off the more attractive concept of a form of theory that has meaning for life. In respect to history he contents himself with the demand that it should throw off its methodological strait jacket even at the cost of losing possible objectivity. And he would like to pacify himself with the reflection that "it is not the victory of *science* that distinguishes our nineteenth century but the victory of the scientific *method* over science." [Habermas adds a footnote to the effect that "Gadamer's philosophical hermeneutics still unavowedly obeys this intention."][17]

Habermas points out that, according to Nietzsche's notion of perspectivism, any arbitrary "illusion"—including the "illusion" of science itself—may appear to be as valid as any other if it fulfills some real need in the world. When the relation of knowledge and interest is understood so naturalistically, the appearance of objectivity dissolves—as Nietzsche intends—but at the same time knowledge becomes subjective (*EI* 361).

Like Nietzsche, however, Gadamer in fact attacks not science itself but a false understanding of science. As we have seen, Gadamer himself discovers that Nietzsche is caught in the same false picture Nietzsche himself attacks. Habermas does an injustice to Gadamer's view by reducing it beyond contextualism to such a subjectivism. Habermas claims that the unveiling of "erkenntnisleitende Interessen" (interests that condition knowledge) is necessary to secure a pragmatic kind of objectivity (see *EI* 360). A defender of Gadamer can readily reply, however, that Gadamer's hermeneutics insists upon precisely such an unveiling over against a naive, theoretical objectivism. Again, the self-understanding of hermeneutics need not be subjective. Rather, it can be intersubjective, with the purpose, for instance, of unveiling knowledge-orienting interests, the methodological presuppositions of a particular interpretive method in the humanities or research program in the social and natural sciences.

Despite Habermas's disagreement with Gadamer on the lack of a sufficiently critical attitude toward the authority of the tradition, there is, of course, a certain amount of agreement, especially on the shortcomings of historical objectivism as a methodological ideal. Habermas allies himself and Gadamer together with Arthur Danto who claims in his book, *Analytical Philosophy of History,* that "we cannot consistently have a complete historical account."[18] Like Gadamer, Danto labels as fiction the concept of historical analysis as two separate and distinct projects—a project of giving a perfect descriptive account and a subsequent project of interpretation. In the spirit of hermeneutics Danto rejects not only the ideal of the "perfect historian"—a machine programmed to be the perfect eyewitness and to give pure historical descriptions—but also the ideal of the "last historian"—a person at the end of history who would thus possess the overarching conception that could then illuminate the truth of all preceding events.

Habermas, however, parts ways with both Danto and Gadamer precisely at this juncture in that he sees a necessity for projecting an ideal understanding—in this case, the overarching conception of a universal history—before the historian can interpret the past at all. On this point he thinks that Wolfhart Pannenberg's critique of Gadamer is on the right track.[20] A close examination of Pannenberg's critique, however, makes it clear that if Habermas really agrees with Gadamer as to the shortcomings of objectivism, he cannot rightfully side with Pannenberg.

Pannenberg essentially agrees with Gadamer that Hegel goes too far in trying to subsume history under absolute self-consciousness. Both Gadamer and Pannenberg emphasize the finitude of human experience. They further agree that interpreters' understanding of the past is conditioned by their understanding of the present, including their expectations about the future. Where the two part ways is in Pannenberg's insistence that the horizon of the present includes a projection of a universal history.[21]

Gadamer shares Danto's suspicions of the unhistorical character of a theory of universal history inherent in the notion of a "last historian." Their reasons for taking this line are similar: the statement (Aussage) of the historical account is always inadequate to its subject matter. Danto explains this by the fact that we cannot know the future, while Gadamer claims the reason to be that the statement is embedded in a context of questions. A question is not verifiable like a statement or proposition. On Gadamer's account, then, historiography is more open to alternative explanations and interpretations than would be allowed by a substantive theory of history with its projection of a final truth to history.

Pannenberg prefaces his defense of universal history with an attack on Gadamer's devaluation of the assertive proposition (Aussage). Following Heidegger, Gadamer argues against the philosophical tradition that takes the declarative proposition as the only form for the proper expression of knowledge. The proposition is objective because it objectifies; it lifts a thing out of its context and makes it stand alone as an object before a consciousness. At least this is the way the relation has been understood, and Pannenberg agrees with this picture when he accepts the argument that "the ability to *objectify,* to grasp the reality confronting one in its (only relative, more or less extensive) independence from experiencing subjectivity, characterizes the human relation to the world, namely, man's specific objectivity based on his far-reaching freedom from instinctual drives" ("HU" 114). Pannenberg's coupling of universal history and objectifying language implies that subjectivity is to be overcome by making completely explicit (in statements) the understanding of the present in a theory that then mediates the interpretation of the past in terms of the present and future.

Gadamer argues in reply that the hermeneutic awareness is more a question of *Sein* than of *Bewusstsein*—of being than of consciousness. By this he means to deny that such an objectification of self-consciousness is possible or desirable and that understanding does not suffer as a result.

The reflection of a given preunderstanding [Vorverständnis] brings something before me that would otherwise happen behind my back. Something—not everything. For hermeneutic awareness [wirkungsgeschichtliches Bewusstsein] is in an unavoidable manner more being than consciousness. That does not mean, however, that it could escape without constantly making ideological torpidity conscious. Only through this reflection am I no longer unfree vis-à-vis myself, but rather am able to decide freely about the justice or injustice of my preunderstandings. [*KS* I 127]

Even though this reflection is essential, it is conditioned by a set of interests that transcends the objectification of a particular result of reflection by allowing for and being open to new experiences and the building of new *Vorverständnisse*. This emphasis on productive openness has as its linguistic corollary Gadamer's argument that the objectifying assertion (Aussage) is not the only form of language in which meaning and understanding can be properly said to be present. Language has other uses, and such uses do not need to be reduced to a dependency on the factual meaning represented in propositions.

In his essay "Was ist Wahrheit?" (*KS* I) Gadamer writes, rather strongly, "I believe one can say in principle that there can be no assertion [Aussage] that is absolutely true" (*KS* I 53). His probable intention is to say that the meaning of the proposition is not just a function of objective reference or of some picture of the world that it presents. Rather, the proposition depends on its relation to other features, such as its historical context and its usefulness in a given situation. Gadamer therefore modifies the claim about the objectivity of the *Aussage*.

There is no assertion [Aussage] that one can grasp only through the content it presents if one wants to grasp it in its truth. Every assertion is motivated. Every assertion has presuppositions that it does not assert.   [*KS* I 54]

This emphasis on the motivation of the assertion need not be interpreted naturalistically; "motivation" does not necessarily mean subjective needs or instincts. The motivation that Gadamer is speaking about is itself linguistic, since he is speaking about the use of such an assertion in terms of the cognitive *question* it answers. Thus the difficulty with *universal* history is that it is too material and substantive. It hardens into a definite answer what basically exists as an open question. The argument for universal history turns a methodological consideration into a demand for a definite method, but this shift subverts the hermeneutic intention of interpreting historiography as a questioning process.

All that Gadamer's metahermeneutics acknowledges about universal history is that any contemporary historical consciousness will also involve an awareness of its own future ("R" 77). This acknowledgment is not a concession, however. It says little more than that some attitude toward the future is an essential dimension of any understanding of the past. Nothing is said about how the future must be conceived. Thus, Gadamer's analysis deals more with "historicity" than with history, and more with "futuricity" than with the future. His philosophical concern is a transcendental one in searching for the underlying conditions for the possibility of thinking about history or about the future.

Some philosophers will find this transcendental, metahermeneutical claim rather empty, but they will also run into difficulties in attempting to specify more concrete and normative appropriateness conditions. In the social sciences, for instance, it appears to some that the appeal to material appropriateness conditions such as "class struggle" and "rational society" may be necessary to guarantee the legitimacy of criticism.

Habermas is one who searches for such a guarantee, but of a transcendental, not a material, sort. One of his basic objections to Gadamer is that criticism is impossible unless the concrete situation in which we stand can be tested against some rational principles as an ideal measure of reason. He turns to models like linguistics and psychoanalysis for such principles—psychoanalysis largely because it shows how barriers that prevent real communication can be overcome, and linguistics because the "communicative competence" of the "ideal speaker" explains the possibility of discourse in general.

For Habermas to make his case in these early essays, he believes he must refute Gadamer's claim that hermeneutics has universal application to all spheres of human behavior. This claim for the universality of hermeneutics depends on the notion that all understanding takes place through language, or what Gadamer calls "linguisticality" (Sprachlichkeit). Gadamer puts this idea rather provocatively when he emphasizes, "*Sein, das verstanden werden kann, ist Sprache*"—being that can be understood is language (*WM* 450). Since hermeneutics is precisely the way language itself is investigated, hermeneutic reflection underlies man's every attempt to think through the relation of language and world. Because hermeneutic reflection involves the critical movement that attempts to clarify and make explicit the preunderstandings involved in discourse (although complete transparence of meaning, as in Hegelian absolute knowledge, is not considered attainable), hermeneutics is essentially *Sprachkritik*.

In these earlier discussions Habermas criticizes Gadamer for emphasizing linguisticality to such an extent. He argues that language is merely one aspect of reality and that other constitutive factors exist. "The objective connection through which alone social actions can be comprehended is constituted out of language, work, and power especially" (*ZLS* 179). This subordination of language by the inclusion of other components presupposes a theoretical realism according to which language is seen as grounded in something other than itself. This theory of language considers language as the reflection, albeit a distorted one, of some underlying prelinguistic reality.

This realism, however, fails to account for the ways that even the modes of work and power must be brought to language and understood in order to be asserted to be constitutive forces. "Language" is not of the same order as power. Rather, it is what enables us to construe the world under these forces. Habermas's objection to Gadamer might be telling against a transcendental model that is idealistic in a Hegelian sense and not hermeneutic and historical. Yet Gadamer rightly refuses to be interpreted as an idealist. In fact, he turns out to be more of a pragmatist, protesting Habermas's imputation that *Truth and Method* advances the idealist claim that language constitutes the world or, in Habermas's words, "that the linguistically articulated consciousness determines the material being of practical life [Lebenspraxis]" (*ZLS* 179). Gadamer's view, like Heidegger's, is that language and world are conterminous, and that both are historical in their appearance:

Nobody will deny that the practical application of modern science fundamentally changes our world and therewith also our language. But precisely: "also our language." That in no way means, as Habermas imputes to me, that the linguistically articulated consciousness determines the material being of practical life [Lebenspraxis]. It only means that there is no social reality with all its real coercions that for its part does not get represented again in a linguistically articulated consciousness. Reality does not happen "behind the back of language" (179), but rather behind the back of the person who lives with the subjective belief that he understands the world (or no longer understands it). Reality also happens in language. [*KS* I 125-126]

Habermas's own later shift toward a linguistic theory of communication as the basis for a *universal* pragmatics (much like Gadamer's *Sprachlichkeit* is the basis for a *universal* hermeneutics) vindicates Gadamer's reply. As long as Gadamer's statement that *"Sein, das verstanden werden kann, ist Sprache"* is not taken as implying a constitutive idealism, the idea is a feasible one. It is not that language reflects thought or is "prior" to the world in some way, but rather that both language and world appear together—as one changes, so does the other. Thus Gadamer claims that language is "the behavior of the world itself in which we live" (*WM* 419). The problem of reflection, of the antithetical relation of mind and world, subject and object, is transcended. The world is not an independent object *for* language; rather, "the world presents itself *in* language" (*WM* 426; emphasis added).

Habermas also argues that Gadamer's emphasis on the tradition is too trusting toward the established language and the ideological values deceptively hidden therein. In *Knowledge and Human Interests,* he fully believes that the psychoanalytic model can be extended to the social sphere. Without the possibility of emancipation from coercion along the order of a psychoanalytic cure, he argues, the language we use will continue to deceive us.

Freud, however, already recognized the difficulties of extending psychoanalysis to the social sphere. At the end of *Civilization and Its Discontents,* he raised the question of the valid extent of the analogy between the individual and the cultural community.

But we should have to be very cautious and not forget that, after all, we are only dealing with analogies and that it is dangerous, not only with men but also with concepts, to tear them from the sphere in which they have originated and been evolved. Moreover, the diagnosis of communal neurosis is faced with a special difficulty. In an individual neurosis we take as our starting point the contrast that distinguishes the patient from his environment, which is assumed to be "normal." For a group all of whose members are affected by one and the same disorder no such background could exist; it would have to be found elsewhere. And as regards the therapeutic application of our knowledge, what would be the use of the most correct analysis of social neuroses, since no one possesses the authority to impose such a therapy upon the group?[22]

Furthermore, it may well be asked where the concept of "normal" is going to come from. What is the ideal viewpoint? Faced with the question of the final value of human civilization and the course of cultural development, Freud's pessimism about progress and about any ideal resolution—about the success of positive, material appropriateness conditions—keeps him from taking a stand. His apology nevertheless contains a very penetrating insight into the desire for such conditions:

Thus I have not the courage to rise up before my fellow-men as *a prophet,* and I bow to their reproach *that I can offer them no consolation: for at bottom that is what they are all demanding*—the wildest revolutionaries no less passionately than the most virtuous believers.[23]

To cite a caution from Freud is, of course, not to refute Habermas. If the argument were intended to refute, it would be a fallacious argument from authority. Since the very question at stake is precisely that of the validity of an appeal to the authority of tradition, to use such an argument would be to compound the fallacy by begging the question as well. The Freud citation emphasizes the very problem of the source of the authority for legitimizing interpretations. To Gadamer, who shares the apparently healthy skepticism of Freud, the ideal authority Habermas sees in a theory of truth as a counterfactual consensus conflicts with the reality of actual practice. Gadamer believes that to adopt, as Habermas does, the notion of a purely rational consensus of the sort that would be possible only if social interaction were completely free from coercions overlooks an important practical difference between the personal sphere and the social sphere. In psychoanalysis the patient is to be cured of his deviation, and accordingly submits to the authority of the analyst. However, in social interaction between groups with different interests, argues Gadamer, "deviation" from the norm of one group is not necessarily a sickness, for the norm itself is what is in question (see "R" 308).

In the last word so far in the Habermas-Gadamer debate—the new postscript to the third edition of *Wahrheit und Methode*—Gadamer continues to be skeptical about Habermas's "overestimation" of the role and effect of philosophical reflection in social reality (*WM* 529). Gadamer can accept the ideal of emancipation as continually generating new goals, and thus belonging to the step-by-step development of historical and social life. But precisely when this ideal is posited as the idea of a completed reflection, it becomes empty and undialectical (*WM* 533). To think that the emancipatory reflection actually leads to the completely rational individual or society overlooks the way dissolving some distorting power relations and constraints is achieved only through instituting others (*WM* 534). Gadamer fears that Habermas is another Robespierre, preaching an abstract, rational morality. He reminds us that the hour eventually comes when society must be freed from such a reign of reason.

Whether Gadamer's fears and reservations are appropriate is a question that must wait for the further development of Habermas's philosophical program. While their debate may indicate a future split in the direction of hermeneutical philosophy—with an insistence upon the transcendental scope of hermeneutics on the one hand, and upon its historicist character on the other—it serves for the present to illustrate two particular aspects of Gadamer's current formulation of his position. The first has to do with the notion of tradition, the second with the relation of hermeneutic criticism to actual *praxis.*

To take the first point, Gadamer explicitly argues that the "tradition" to which all understanding relates is not merely the actual historical state of affairs or the established privileges and values. On the contrary, what is involved is more like Nietzsche's "critical history." This kind of history, as Heidegger points out in *Being and Time,* involves a reflective move of detachment from the present; this movement is crucial for Heidegger if historical reflection is to be authentic (see *SZ* 397). The detachment is both a disavowal of what many in the present take to be the meaning of their heritage and an affirmation of whatever in the past is taken as one's true heritage and as a valid and practicable possibility for the future (see *SZ* 386).

Gadamer does not mention Nietzsche or Heidegger in this regard, but his dialectical understanding of the notion of tradition is clearly very similar. In reply to misunderstandings of this notion, Gadamer notes:

In this idea there is in no way a preference for the conventional, to which one must then blindly subjugate oneself. The phrase "connection with the tradition" [Anschluss an die Tradition] means, rather, only that tradition is not merely what one knows to be and is conscious of as one's own origins, so that tradition cannot be preserved [aufgehoben] in an adequate historical consciousness. Changing the established forms is no less a kind of connection with the tradition than defending the established forms. Tradition exists only in constant alteration. "To gain a connection" [Anschluss gewinnen] with the tradition is a formulation intended to call attention to an experience whereby our plans and wishes are always in advance of reality, and are, so to speak, even without connection with reality. What then becomes important is to mediate between desirable anticipations and practicable possibilities, between sheer wishes and actual intentions—that is, to imagine the anticipations in the substance of reality.   ["R" 307]

This statement shows the appeal to tradition to be *pragmatic* rather than *dogmatic.* As such, it is not intended to preserve old standards and methods of interpretations, nor the old results.

It might be inferred that Gadamer leaves us with the revolutionary conclusion that anything at all can be said, that the tradition can be claimed by any view or interpretation. This view grows out of the fact that even a total revaluation of the tradition (after the fashion of Heidegger's inversion and "destruction" of the history of metaphysics) can be carried out in the name of that very tradition—as the real "truth" of the tradition to which everybody else has been blind. This is not a totally absurd result, as will be argued (with important qualifications), but it does not follow necessarily from Gadamer's theory precisely because of the pragmatic emphasis. The interpretation must relate, even if by contrast, to the tradition, to the work's or the idea's history of effects (Wirkungsgeschichte). Because of this essential connection, the interpretation, if it is to understand its own force and validity, must become cognizant of the way it relates to this tradition and the way in which traditional preconceptions may still be working themselves out in this very interpretation.

Though relation to tradition is itself an essential appropriateness condition, it does not function in the normatively dogmatic way that Hirsch and Habermas have understood. Rather, the appeal to tradition demands the possibility of criticism: it requires a move to methodological self-consciousness, to awareness of the relation between what is being said and what should be said.

Instead of being yet another method, Gadamer's hermeneutics is a call for methodical self-reflection on the part of all the humanistic enterprises. In that sense, however, hermeneutics is still essentially linked to praxis. Another major question involved in the Habermas-Gadamer debate, therefore, hinges on the relation of hermeneutic criticism and actual praxis.

IV. SUMMARY: HERMENEUTICS AS CRITIQUE

What kind of knowledge knows the difference between theoretical knowledge and practical knowledge? In criticism of Plato, Aristotle in the *Nicomachean Ethics* argues that purely theoretical knowledge of the good will not lead to the good life—such a knowledge is empty in comparison to the practical understanding embedded in actual situations. Yet there is a further distinction between the mere technical know-how (techne) involved in, say, the politician's management of the state and the practical understanding (phronesis) of the *true* statesman who understands the principles involved. What kind of knowledge allows Aristotle to distinguish between *phronesis* and *techne?*

Gadamer poses these questions in his "Replik," for they must also be asked of hermeneutics itself. Hermeneutics clearly cannot be opposed to *techne* as such since it is only through the production of an interpretation that a text comes to be understood. If hermeneutic reflection appears to be critical of particular forms *techne* has taken (of "methods" and "approaches"), this criticism is aimed at the self-understanding involved, or, more likely, at the lack of self-understanding involved. The politician may succeed in some political affairs, but insofar as his activity is not accompanied by reflection on principles, his knowledge of the reasons for his success is incomplete and his attainments only temporary. While philosophical critique does not necessarily deal with particular political strategies, it can lead to a beneficial clarification of political principles. Similarly, Gadamer's hermeneutic critique of technology and science does not attack science as a whole (see "R" 283). It is not "antiscientific" to clarify the scope, basis, and assumptions of scientific enterprises, especially of the social and humanistic sciences.

Thus, although hermeneutics can be closely connected with *techne*—that is, with the actual ongoing inquiries and interpretations—its level of generality is nevertheless distinct. Hermeneutics can elucidate the kind of conditions involved in inquiry and in communication in general, but it cannot go so far as to establish particular sociopolitical convictions (for example, that society is structured by class struggles) as necessary facts or norms.

In general, since hermeneutic theory is philosophy and not a particular science (like philology, for instance), it cannot supply material appropriateness conditions for interpretive contexts. It cannot be so tied to practice that it can legislate a canon of interpretive norms or a doctrine, "school," or "method" of criticism. Nevertheless, it has an essential connection with practice, for it is concerned with a special class of appropriateness conditions, including those discussed by *philosophy* in its questions about how we can be said to have certain knowledge, about how sentences can be said to be true, and about how utterances can be said to be meaningful.

The kind of knowledge or understanding involved in hermeneutic reflection is itself neither strictly theoretical nor strictly practical. Aristotle himself, Gadamer points out, recognized that his own students required a certain degree of maturity and an under-

standing of their society and situation before they could understand not only the philosophical discussion itself—which, by its
generality, necessitates a distancing of oneself from one's actual
situation—but also its value for and application to the life for
which they as future citizens were being educated. Hermeneutics,
then, like Aristotle's practical science, is not *techne* or *Lehre*
("doctrine" in the sense of Schleiermacher's hermeneutics). It is
essentially philosophical *Kritik* ("R" 287).

Criticism implies distance, and the distance introduced by the
generality of philosophical reflection makes possible the negative
move essential to criticism. But criticism must also be able to return constructively, and here greater methodological self-awareness makes actual interpretations more self-consistent and hence
more legitimate. Finally, hermeneutics also contributes a basis for
arbitration between different interpretations by demanding that
the extent to which the interpretation has clarified its own assumptions and scope—and has remained consistent with those assumptions and within that scope—be made a further test for the interpretation. Hermeneutics should not, however, legislate a priori the
range of assumptions that can actually work or the kinds of contexts into which the text can be introduced but must investigate
each development as it comes along.

FIVE
Hermes and Clio

I. LITERARY HISTORY: PARADOX OR PARADIGM?

In an essay discussing the constitutive force of modern science for modern thought, Martin Heidegger identifies a shortcoming of the historical sciences.

> The sphere of historical research extends only so far as historical explanation reaches. The unique, the rare, the simple—in short, the great—in history is never self-evident and hence remains unexplainable.... Nor is there any other historical explanation so long as explanation means reduction to the intelligible, and so long as history remains research, that is, explanation.[1]

If this description in fact characterizes modern historical research, then the enterprise of *literary* history is an impossible one. For if explanation can only be reductive, proceeding exclusively by comparison of repeatable types of occurrences, the unique and unrepeatable quality of the literary work, its specifically poetic value, cannot be reached by historical research. Furthermore, if explaining a literary work historically means comparing it with other works in order to reveal a sequence, the immanent uniqueness of the work as literature is denied insofar as the work is reduced to a sociohistorical product of its antecedents and its milieu. The literary artwork thus has no place in history, and history can only be puzzled by literature.

This paradox raises difficult questions about the methodological foundations of literary criticism—questions that literary critics have not avoided. Roland Barthes, in his essay "Histoire ou littérature?," published with his own literary historical study *Sur Racine* (Paris: Seuil, 1963), confronts the paradox boldly. He argues that literary history has largely been a result of confusing the methods of historical research with those of psychological study. This confusion has generated, not a history of the literary works but a history of the writers. His attack on the traditional program of psychological reconstruction of the author's intentions and historical setting goes so far that it leads to the slogan "Amputer la littérature de l'individu!" (*SR* 156). Instead of revitalizing the concept of literary history, however, he is willing to accept the limitations of historical research methods and asks history only for a history of the functions of literature: "It is then only at the level of literary functions (production, communication, consumption) that history can place itself, and not at the level of the individuals who carried them out" (*SR* 155-156). Barthes thus grants that from the historical point of view the literary work is necessarily only a document, the trace of a larger activity to be reconstructed. His formalist program has therefore not changed an essentially reductivist and scientistic understanding of literary history; it has merely assigned it another sphere of research: the material relations and conditions of literature as a social institution. Barthes admits that in this reduction of the scope of literary history, *literary* history disappears in becoming just history. Here again, the concepts "literature" and "history" are understood in such a way that "literary history" becomes an impossible enterprise.

The paradox is not restricted to Barthes's understanding of the terms. Geoffrey Hartman in his book *Beyond Formalism* (New Haven: Yale University Press, 1970) poses the dilemma as a general one.

Thus the formality of art becomes a central issue in any literary history. How do we ground art in history without denying its autonomy, its aristocratic resistance to the tooth of time? [P. 358]

The antinomy involved in the notion of literary history is generated by both the indubitable immanence of the poetic text and the equally incontestable historical dimension it acquires as the subject of interpretation in time. The transitory character of the interpretations, with their dependence on historical perspectives that are continually transcended, contrasts pointedly with the endurance of the poetic work. A practical theory of literary interpretation must come to terms with the tension between the immanence of literature and the historicity of interpretation.

At present at least two general theories of interpretation have emerged which take contrary stands on the problem. On the one hand, Barthes's structuralist theory, which aims at generating a science of literature, appears to be radically formalistic and antihistorical. On the other hand, Gadamer's philosophical hermeneutics, following Heidegger's analysis of the temporality of understanding, insists that art is essentially historical. Gadamer's philosophy approaches the paradox of historicity and immanence in a way that makes literary history of paradigmatic importance, and his views have been developed at the level of practical criticism into a theory emphasizing reception and influence. Given the paradox the structuralist or formalist inevitably sees in the notion of history, the question is whether hermeneutic theory and related approaches to practical criticism can provide an alternative theoretical, methodological account that will clear the way for the actual practice of literary history.

II. BEYOND HISTORICISM?

In order to come to a clearer understanding of the general problem, it will be helpful to reflect historically and to investigate the problem as it arose in the consciousness of a thinker who was himself both a philosopher and a philologist. As a philologist, Friedrich Nietzsche was at once sharply critical of his profession and deeply convinced of the value of disciplined reading of texts.[2] Given such a self-critical attitude, his task as a philosopher became one of clarifying the methodological and epistemological base on which the interpretive mind could establish the validity of its historical reflections. Yet for Nietzsche it was not sufficient to speak of the validity of knowledge, and thus in his essay "On the Use and Disadvantage of History for Life'' he explores the question of the value of historical reflection for the life-context in which it originates.

This essay challenges and unmasks the tendency of Nietzsche's own time to sink into historical reflection to such an extent that it can no longer emerge from its preoccupation with the past in order to engage itself in real *life,* in the active task of creating a future (*UB* 242). The tension between the reflective, historical spirit and the creative, artistic life is portrayed along the lines of the more general dialectical relation between reflection and spontaneity. Reflection poses a danger for spontaneous action in that it can reveal so many reasons and causes and pose so many possible alternatives that its effect is debilitating. In Nietzsche's language, in order to act creatively one has to learn to forget. Man, unlike the herd animal, is the creature that remembers, but such remembering produces only regret (*UB* 244-245). Similarly, the more a creative spirit, such as an artist, reflects on his historical antecedents and consequences, the less likely he is to think of himself as original and creative. Creativity requires a break with the past and with the constraints the past imposes on artistic spontaneity. The difficulty is that man as a reflective being cannot simply return to a state of pure immediacy. The modern irony is that only through reflection can the problem of reflection be resolved (*UB* 302).

Nietzsche himself attempts to deal with the problem by delegating the task of forgetting history and active creation to a future generation called "youth" (*UB* 320 f.). In his essay "Literary History and Literary Modernity," Paul de Man incisively notes the *mauvaise foi* in this move. De Man's reading of the essay interprets the conflict between the reflectivity of *history* and the creativity involved in *life* as essentially "modern"—that is, not only characteristic of recent times but also constitutive of the very notion of modernity. Modernity and history are locked together in eternal irony: "If history is not to become sheer regression or paralysis, it depends on modernity for its duration and renewal; but modernity cannot assert itself without being at once swallowed up and reintegrated into a regressive historical process." For de Man this irony is not only the essence of modernity, but of literature as such, for "literature has always been essentially modern." In de Man's reading Nietzsche's paradox becomes not a problem to be resolved, but a description of the modern predicament per se, one that is an inescapable feature of literary writing.[3]

While de Man's analysis provides a valuable insight into the concept of modernity, the question remains whether affirming the tension to be a necessary state of affairs does not perpetuate metaphysical assumptions and an ironic cynicism that Nietzsche correctly attempted to undercut and overcome. Heidegger, for instance, in a very Nietzschean analysis in *Holzwege* (p. 85), suggests that the world view in which the age sees itself as new, or modern, represents a decision to see the world as a view and is tied to a self-understanding of man as *subjectum*. The project then becomes one of changing this self-understanding, not just of repeating it. Heidegger's discussion is one way of continuing Nietzsche's inquiry, although a problematic one. For present purposes it will be more relevant to consider the epistemological problem that concerned Nietzsche in this essay and that still demands clarification.

Nietzsche's critique of historiographical objectivity involves an attack on the objectivist goal of completely abstracting from the perspective of the present and attaining an interest-free picture of the past (*UB* 285 f.). This epistemological question concerning the knowability of the past is accompanied by the moral-psychological concern with the *results* of the objectivist assumptions. Thus Nietzsche accuses objectivism of destroying the horizon of illusions surrounding an age, without which the creativity essential to cultural "life" is impossible (*UB* 291). The methodological model of objectivism involves a decision that the historical past is a self-subsistent and closed horizon objectifiable for purposes of study. An age is a horizon into which the historian transposes himself after having completely suspended the horizon of his own present. But if such self-displacement into another system of perceptions and beliefs were in fact possible, any such system of beliefs would appear to be replaceable by any other. The awareness of the arbitrariness of one's own system of beliefs would itself undercut the ability to believe. For Nietzsche objectivity can conceal a nihilistic relativism that represents an attitude of weakness and an inability to act, a "will to nothingness."[4]

Nietzsche himself, however, has not entirely overcome what he has criticized. The dilemma of the essay on history is partly a false one because he sets positions against each other without com-

pletely accepting or rejecting either one. Nietzsche himself remarks on this method when he notes, "Deeply mistrustful of epistemological dogmas, I loved to look first out of one window and
then out of another, keeping myself from immuring myself in
them, for I considered this harmful."[5] Thus although he rejects
the objectivist self-understanding of scientific historiography, he
proceeds to argue as if this objectivity were in fact realizable, when
on his own grounds knowledge is necessarily rooted in interests
and perspectives. As such, historical knowledge would never be
completely separable from present interests, and the relation between history and life, and between reflection and art, could not
be as antithetical as Nietzsche makes it seem.

The concern of recent hermeneutical philosophy with developing an ontological philosophy of interpretation has had to deal
with Nietzsche's thinking. Gadamer, criticizing Nietzsche's analysis of horizon, objects specifically to Nietzsche's assumption that
the historical past consists of ages, each with its own horizon—
that is, with its own system of perception- and action-orienting beliefs. Like Nietzsche, Gadamer rejects the idea that this transpos-
ing of oneself (Sichversetzen) into the past horizon should or could
involve leaving oneself out of consideration (Von-sich-absehen).
But whereas Nietzsche settles for the empty admonition that a
more youthful generation will have to risk the loss of possible
objectivity by making history more useful to life, Gadamer unmasks the paradox and abandons the model of historical understanding that generated the antinomy in the first place.

With such philosophical antecedents as Husserl's phenomenological notion of horizon and Heidegger's hermeneutical analysis
of understanding, Gadamer's theory can avoid the subject-object
antinomy that generates paradoxes for Nietzsche. Gadamer's philosophical hermeneutics rethinks the *Fragestellung*—the whole
manner of questioning—of traditional poetics and aesthetics. Instead of limiting poetics and aesthetics to a description and deter-
mination of the characteristics of the object of a particular mode
of experiencing, the aesthetic, the hermeneutic questioning challenges the very notion of a purely "aesthetic" experience. The
encounter with the artwork is a project of interpretive understanding, not merely a passive, distanced reception and appreciation of
an independent object. Essential to the understanding of the art-

work is a movement toward self-understanding in the interpreter. Since self-understanding does not take place in a vacuum but involves attaining true beliefs about one's self and situation, philosophical hermeneutics speaks about the *truth,* in the large sense of the term, manifested in art and in history (*WM* 161).

With this emphasis on truth rather than merely on validity, Gadamer breaks away from the formalist assumptions dominating contemporary poetics. Normally present-day philosophers discuss truth only in relation to assertions or statements involving a predication relation. Given this approach, poetry is left in a difficult position. Since poetry often makes false statements or describes nonexistent states of affairs (and thus is neither confirmable nor disconfirmable in a strict sense), it cannot readily be considered as truth. In order to save poetry from the logical status of a lie, poetry can be aestheticized by claiming, as Sir Philip Sidney did, that the poet "nothing affirmeth and therefore never lieth." The poet is thus said simply not to be asserting his statements—that is, not to be claiming any truth for them. Poetry is thereby taken out of the world, out of a historical situation with operant effects (Wirkung), and must be seen from a disinterested distance.

In order to reestablish a way of speaking about the truth, not only of interpretation but also of poetry and art in general, Gadamer must criticize a dominant philosophical aesthetic. Stemming particularly from Kant, this aesthetic subjectivizes art, turning it into an object for a disinterested, purely receptive, aesthetic consciousness (see *WM* 84 ff.). A corresponding aestheticizing of history must also be combatted and replaced by an emphasis on the historicity of art. "Aesthetics," writes Gadamer, "has to be transformed into hermeneutics" (*WM* 157). This dialectical suggestion that hermeneutics is higher and more inclusive means that the philosophical task in thinking about art is no longer to explain the eternal beauty of nature but to clarify the conditions for the process by which art comes to be understood and interpreted. This process takes place in time and in a historical tradition of successive dialogues with the artwork. This tradition must itself be reflected upon if the artwork and the dialogical encounter with the artwork are to be understood. A properly hermeneutical consciousness (wirkungsgeschichtliches Bewusstsein) will be aware of the constitutive force of this tradition. Hence, at the same time that this consciousness believes in the truth it attains by seeing through the distortions of previous interpretations, it will also be aware of its own historicity. The hermeneutic consciousness will therefore be continually forced toward self-reflection, toward an examination of the limits and inadequacies of its own interpretive methods and results.

The reflection on the historical character of art, on the way it generates a tradition of interpretation in which the present itself is rooted, is thus for Gadamer an essential moment of interpretive and creative thinking. His position stands in sharp contrast to Nietzsche's, whose gaze was too firmly fixed on the Medusan image of the danger and paradox of historical reflection. In fact, Gadamer's position can be seen as trying to go beyond Nietzsche precisely by turning paradox into paradigm. In Gadamer's theory this hermeneutical consciousness of the need for historical self-understanding is not only an essential condition of understanding, but also paradigmatic for it. "A truly historical thinking," Gadamer insists, "must also think its own historicity" (*WM* 283).

That this *wirkungsgeschichtliches Bewusstsein*—the hermeneutic awareness that the literary work stands in a tradition of interpretation influencing present understanding—can be called a historicist awareness is clear, but one must be careful to keep the term distinct from a number of possible connotations. The hermeneutic awareness is clearly not historicist in the sense that Hegel and Marx are said to be historicists (for example, by Popper in his idiosyncratic use of the term). The positing of a universal history and a necessary end to historical development, as well as the idea of progress itself, are additional tenets that do not follow from the hermeneutic awareness. They would follow only with additional premises (concerning, for instance, the possibility of absolute knowledge and complete transparency of meaning) that would be denied by the hermeneutic insistence on the finitude and circularity that make interpretation an ongoing task. Furthermore, the strictly methodological hermeneutic reflection does not establish determinate historical values and concrete historical goals and is not a theory aimed at prediction and prophecy.

The hermeneutic version of historicist awareness also does not entail a nihilistic relativism following from a model of the present and the past as circles closed to each other by absolute cultural-temporal differences. Such a model keeps Nietzsche from being able to reconcile historical reflection with active creation. But, as a classical philologist, Nietzsche should have realized that the Muses themselves were the daughters not only of the powerful Zeus but also of Mnemosyne (Memory). And they include not only the Muse of lyric poetry, Euterpe, but also the Muse of history, Clio. Gadamer's hermeneutics denies that past and present, reflection and action, are essentially separate. Instead, he holds that both are elements in a horizon that can be shifted, enlarged, or diminished. Knowledge of the past is not *just* present knowledge, and understanding something does not necessarily mean agreeing with it.

The hermeneutic reflection can thus be described as a historicist reflection aware of its limitations. Sometimes a version of the historicist thesis (such as "all our beliefs, ideas, and theories are subject to change and will change") is taken to imply that we should change our beliefs now. But this is an invalid conclusion—it simply does not follow. We hold our present beliefs because we think they are supported or supportable. We recognize, however, that if new evidence to the contrary arises, we would be willing and likely to change our beliefs. Until that time, there is no reason for not believing what we believe. The belief that beliefs change does not therefore mean that no belief is possible any longer. It merely implies that we should be aware that truths may not be eternal and that we should be willing to change beliefs if we have good reason for such a change. This historicist thesis involves a second-order belief, or a "belief about beliefs" (sometimes called an "attitude" as distinct from a "belief"). As such, to confuse it with first-order beliefs and to draw a nihilistic conclusion from it is fallacious. The hermeneutic reflection combines the historicist thesis with the tenet that the historicist thesis does not necessarily change present beliefs.

The insistence that the connection of understanding to tradition does not preclude criticism is of central importance. The argument for this point shows that the claim for context-bound or tradition-bound understanding does not rule out the possibility of a complete revaluation of previous ways of understanding the historical tradition. The rethinking of the past by T. S. Eliot or Heidegger, for example, is a rejection, not necessarily of tradition per se but of a dominant way of interpreting the tradition. Of course such rethinking may not succeed or be effective in the community of interpretation. It may, however, affect that community simply by bringing about an awareness of the possibility of reinterpretation and, concomitantly, an increased awareness of the way readings of texts are entrenched in a tradition of thought. This increased awareness may allow elements of a reading, previously taken to be absolute facts, suddenly to appear as mere conventions based on entrenched assumptions or evaluations.

This summary discussion suggests that in literary history evaluation plays an essential role, and the task of literary history cannot consist simply of collecting facts about the origins of the literary work. To subsume works under a common heading of a movement or a period is to weigh the relative value of different works to determine which of them are significant enough to define a class. The suggestion that literary history is evaluative can, of course, be countered with the same objection Max Weber made to the charge that sociology is value-laden: it does not follow that an account is itself value-laden from the fact that what the account is giving an account of is value-laden—that is, that the objects of the account are themselves values.

While this observation applies to a subject matter strictly embedded in a conventional vocabulary more univocally defined, it does not protect an enterprise such as literary history. Giving an account of works of art already presupposes an answer to the question of the nature of art. Such an implicit presupposition is problematic not only because opinion varies so widely, but also because it is an essential part of the humanistic-historical enterprise to raise the very question, "What is art?" or "What is literature?" The turn to the past is necessary, then, to see how art or literature has been understood previously. This historical project is tied to and is part of a present question. To think that the literary-historical project has a completely independent validity is to make it into a question-begging enterprise. To recognize it as bound to a present concern with the question "What is literature?" is, of course, to make it a necessarily circular enterprise, but not in any sense fallacious.

That the historical *importance* of literary works is at stake indicates, then, that the literary-historical enterprise is not purely factual. Rather, it is linked to a kind of thinking that makes possible a revaluation of the tradition as such.[6] To understand this possibility, we must inquire about history. Is it merely factual or is it evaluative in any important sense? There is no need to apply methodological requirements to literary history which do not apply to historiography in general. This is not to assume that literary history is merely a *kind* of historiography, a subdivision. Any rethinking of the nature of literary history will also have to question the relation of history and philology (in the broad sense of the term as the study and love of literature). This relation becomes explicitly problematic where the relation of history and literature as normally understood undergoes a radical inversion.

III. "HISTORY OR LITERATURE?" GADAMER CONTRA BARTHES

Gadamer's concept of hermeneutic awareness (wirkungsgeschichtliches Bewusstsein) suggests a revision of the relation of meaning and being in modern poetics. Contrary to the current, even somewhat axiomatic, idea that a poem should not mean but be, Gadamer's analysis suggests that poetry fulfills the desire of language "to be what it means." The implication of this point for a theory of interpretation is that interpretation necessarily places a poem in a context of meaning supplied by the interpreter: "So the interpreting word is the word of the interpreter—it is not the language and lexicon of the interpreted text" (*WM* 448).

Roland Barthes also argues that the context of meaning comes from the critic and not from the text. Like Gadamer, who writes, "All interpretation is one-sided" (*KS* II 194), Barthes argues that no interpretation is "innocent": since the critic is the one who puts the text into a context, it is the critic who decides when "to apply the brakes"—that is, where to draw the boundaries of the context. This argument is advanced in the essay "Histoire ou littérature?" It is almost a French version of Wimsatt and Beardsley's "The Intentional Fallacy," since Barthes debunks the traditional aim of literary studies (especially as carried out by academics in France) to recreate the author's personal self and his setting as he and his contemporaries saw it. His conclusion about literary criticism, however, is exactly opposed to Wimsatt and Beardsley. While they hold that this debunking will lead to more objective criticism, Barthes's radical language suggests that such depsychologizing shows the context as coming from the interpreter and all criticism as being utterly subjective.

Gadamer and Barthes agree on both the contextual nature of interpretation and their opposition to the objectivists. Yet Gadamer does not believe that this position entails the necessary subjectivity of criticism. Depicting the contrasts between Gadamer and Barthes, between hermeneutics and structuralism, will in turn lead to a clarification of the problematic nature of literary history.

Articles by Barthes written after "Histoire ou littérature?" show an understanding of history that is much less reductionist and scientistic than is suggested in his previous account; they throw a proper perspective on his arguments in "Histoire ou littérature?" Thus, in one place he explodes the meaning of "science" as such, noting that in many ways literature is science, and that science (human sciences, and particularly literary study) must become literature (see "Science versus Literature," *The Times Literary Supplement,* 28 September 1967). Concerning the present issue, Barthes provides a provocative account of the literary forms of historiographical writing in "Le Discours de l'histoire" (*Social Science Information,* IV, 4, August 1967). Barthes sees historical narrative as necessarily a form of literature, partly because of the time difference between the subject matter (history) and the language-act of reporting it (the history book).

Barthes, concerned with the literary devices needed to "shift" between the two time scales of the event as it happens and the history as it is written, examines the especially interesting case of those works that go to great lengths to avoid any acknowledgment of an audience or of the historian himself. By suppressing the "I," the history book follows the tactic of certain forms of realist fiction and creates the illusion of objectivity—the illusion that the subject matter is speaking for itself. Other narrative devices used for the same purpose include nominalization (using a single word, such as conspiracy, for a complex of actions), assertion (Barthes finds that the negative statement is rarely used in the historical discourse he analyzes), metaphor, and metonymy. Because the use of linguistic devices is a necessary part of narration, Barthes expresses sympathy with the view that a "fact" is merely a linguistic construct rather than a genuine referent to the real. He quotes favorably Nietzsche's statement that "there are no facts in themselves." Using a linguistic model to restate Nietzsche's point, Barthes maintains that historical discourse of the narrative type is a "fake performative" with "pretensions to 'realism.'" The meaning of the statement that something has occurred is, for Barthes, merely an assertion by someone that the event happened. There is no longer any such thing as "reality" to which historical writing refers; rather, for contemporary history the only ground for the account is the intelligiblity of the account itself. Why some accounts are more intelligible than others, why historians are prima facie more restricted in what they say than poets, and why historical accounts can turn out to be false—all these are problems not discussed by Barthes. They offer serious difficulties for his theories. In reacting to an extreme objectivistic scientism, Barthes tends to fulfill Nietzsche's paradox by falling into extreme historical relativism.

Barthes's earlier essay "Histoire ou littérature?" also raises the specter of relativism by suggesting that alternative approaches, of which there are "thousands," cannot be contested. In *Critique et vérité* Barthes defends his notion against the accusation made by his opponent Raymond Picard that so radically subjectivistic an enterprise allows "anything at all" to be said about the text (*CV* 64). Barthes rebuts this criticism by maintaining that there are necessary constraints on literary interpretation: "exhaustivité" (the potential to explicate all the phrases of the work); the logic of the textual symbols themselves; and finally, the constraint, placed on interpretive language by itself, of internal consistency (*CV* 63 f.).

This rebuttal is surely adequate to Picard's accusation, but the objection itself is stated so broadly ("*anything* at all") that Barthes only needs to point out *some* necessary restriction to make his case. He is, of course, quite right in maintaining that the traditional criteria of coherence and inclusiveness constrain the interpretive enterprise, but these are purely formal and rather minimal restrictions. More has to be said, especially since, on Barthes's account, these constraints appear to be unrealizable ideals. In his own terms criticism is never more than a "périphrase"—that is, an incomplete circumlocution (*CV* 72). In rebelling against the traditional model of interpretation according to which the text is an object about which something "true" is to be said, Barthes has discarded the whole idea that the interpretation corresponds to the literary text. In *Essais critiques* (Paris: Seuil, 1964), he goes so far as to reject the possibility of speaking about the "truth" of an interpretation, holding that interpretation can be syntactically valid—that is, consistent or coherent—but not true—that is, not verifiable (*EC* 255). The discourse of criticism finds an analogical paradigm in formal logic, Barthes believes, because both are "purely formal, not in the aesthetic sense but in the logical sense of the term"; that is, both are "never more than tautological" (*EC* 256).

Since Gadamer's hermeneutic philosophy continues to speak of truth in interpretation, it must of necessity resist Barthes's rhetorical rejection of the vocabulary of truth (or at least of a kind of truth that is more than tautological). Before analyzing this dissension, however, it should be pointed out that the hermeneutic theory and the structuralist theory are in agreement in a number of ways, especially on the criticism to be leveled against previous methodological assumptions of literary theory. Both carry out thoroughgoing criticism of objectivity in interpretation, emphasizing that the context of meaning into which the text is put comes from the critic and not merely from the text alone. Both also reject the psychologistic model whereby the meaning of the text is strictly determined by the intentions of a subject, the author. Finally, both refute a restrictive philological methodology that limits literary history to the task of merely recreating the original horizon of the text, of reading the text only as it was originally read.

As in the case of Nietzsche, however, Barthes's criticism of the traditional methods of philology does not appear to free him from the language that produced the original antinomies. The rejection of the correspondence theory of truth results only in the use of such terms as "coherence," "intelligiblity," and "validity"—the vocabulary of traditional coherence theories of truth. The process does not overcome the ills of objectivism; it merely generates its dialectical opposite: a relativism that denies the possibility of the truth of a subject matter and which suggests a retreat into a purely aesthetic contemplation of syntactical possibilities. The suggestion that historical writing is merely one form of intelligible literature tends to turn history into an aesthetic enterprise whereby the history writer or researcher merely "creates" the "story" he wants to tell. Such accounts, which leave out an important dimension of interpretation, are not an adequate description of the process of understanding. In the case of history, the account overlooks the compelling claim of an understanding of the past on the present and the force of this understanding in determining the activity of peoples and nations. History is in fact usually taken to be not only a possibly valid or intelligible description, but a true actuality. In the case of literary interpretation the danger arises that when the dimension of truth is eliminated and meaning is reduced to claims that are merely intelligible and coherent, interpretation threatens to be valid but thin.

In sharp contrast with the formalistic reduction that rejects the possibility of truth in interpretation stands Gadamer's insistence not only on the immanence of the text but also on the expectation of the truth of what the text says: "There is presupposed not only an immanent unity of meaning [immanente Sinneinheit] that gives the reader direction, but also transcendent expectations of meaning [transzendenten Sinnerwartungen] that constantly guide the reader's comprehension" (*WM* 278). In reply to Barthes, the hermeneutic position can point out that rejection of a correspondence theory of truth does not necessarily lead to a total relinquishing of the concept of truth. Gadamer's hermeneutics finds belief in the truth of the interpretive understanding to be an essential moment without which understanding as such is impossible. A text is not an object in itself, to be viewed from various perspectives or in different profiles; rather, it is the product of a dialogue directed by the expectation that something meaningful is said *about* something. This expectation is in turn a motivation for treating the text as an immanent, self-contained system of meaning—for approaching it with what Gadamer calls the anticipation of perfection. On the hermeneutic account, then, immanence and truth must be seen not only as properties of the text, but also as assumptions granted to the text by the reader in the process of letting the text speak for itself. The text does not exist except in a dialogue between text and interpreter.

The expectation of truth is not a self-confirming hypothesis. In the reading process the preunderstandings with which the text is first approached are confirmed or falsified in the course of the reader's dialogue with the text. The ability of understanding to correct itself indicates that it is not relative in a vicious way and that all reading involves some truth-awareness. The very fact that the historical-philological disciplines have successful ways of avoiding error in interpretation provides hermeneutics with phenomenological evidence for an awareness of the possibility of a truth of the subject matter (*WM* xix). Relativism is not a threat for hermeneutic theory precisely because understanding is a learning process in which criticism (of students, for example, or as self-criticism in the form of self-correction) does in fact occur.

IV. THE COMMON NATURE OF HISTORICAL AND LITERARY TEXTS

The hermeneutic position insists that every reading of a text contains an underlying subject matter (Sache) to which the text refers and which guides the comprehension of the reader to an understanding that can be said to be true. The objection can be raised that emphasis on the *Sache* is more appropriate to such texts as historical documents than to poetic texts, since the latter are held to be strictly immanent, referring only to themselves. For Gadamer, however, the distance between history texts and literary texts is not as great as is ordinarily thought, though his rapprochement of the two genres of writing takes the opposite tack from that of Barthes. Gadamer does not remove the transcendent reference to a subject matter from historical writing; rather, he maintains that this signifying movement occurs in *both* literature and history, although in different ways.

Does Gadamer's argument for the close connection between these two kinds of texts run the danger of doing both an injustice? There are obvious prima facie differences between the historian's treatment of a particular document and the literary critic's approach to a literary text. The historian uses the text to find out about something other than the text—an event, a belief, a mental or physical state, and the like. The critic, for his part, recognizes the immanence of the literary text. The historian is not necessarily interested in the text's own indication of intention; he wants to know the truth, which is not necessarily what the text implies as true. From that point of view he can suspend the truth-claim of the text altogether and read the text simply to know what it states. This suspension, however, seems to have become paradigmatic for modern scholars. Rather than representing a minimal reading, it is taken as the goal of all reading, including the reading of literary texts. The question arises whether such a suspension is characteristic of the historian's project as such.

Here Gadamer answers with a definite "no," offering an interesting contribution to current methodological debate among philosophers of history about the historian's activity (see especially *WM* 317-325). Gadamer argues that the historian's willingness to let the text be interpreted in terms of a concrete reality that transcends it is made possible by the hermeneutic awareness that accompanies the historian's view of the historical horizon. In other words, because the historian is aware that the text is itself historically conditioned and might not contain the truth of the situation, he is able to widen or narrow the scope of the context that he applies in reading the text. The minimal kind of reading—wanting to know merely what is there—is the result of such a narrowing. It cannot be maintained for long, lest the significance of what is being said, and even the very understanding of what *is* said, escape. Although the historian does not consider himself the direct *addressee* of the text—as the reader of a literary text must if the text claims him directly as literature—the historian is concerned with knowing the truth of the matter. In this he joins the reader of literature who is also concerned with the truth of the subject matter (form *or* content) of the text. The historian widens his context in order to determine how the historical situation as a whole, and not merely the particular document, should be understood as soon as the document is found to misrepresent the actual situation—that is, as soon as the text is interpreted in a fashion different from its own intention. The historian must additionally decide how to interpret a variety of texts and how to interpret the reconstructed situation in terms of preceding and subsequent developments as construed from still other documents.

The task of the historian is to determine "the historiographical meaning of a phenomenon in the whole of its historical self-consciousness" (*WM* 321). The historian is thus trying to interpret the "text" of a historical period or epoch. Furthermore, he is captured by this larger "text" in the same way that occurs in every genuine reading:

> In truth there is never a reader before whose eyes the big book of world history simply lies there opened. But there is also never a reader who, when he has the text before his eyes, simply reads what stands there. Rather, in all reading there occurs an application, so that whoever reads a text is also himself caught up in the meaning in question. He listens along with the text that he understands.
>
> [*WM* 323]

The historian, caught up in history, runs the risk of forgetting himself and his own historicity in dealing with the unity of the past and with a tradition in which he himself stands. In that sense, the historian's task is more like the literary critic's than like the natural scientist's, since the historian is claimed by the "text" he interprets in a particular way and his understanding is conditioned by that very "text." Both literary critic and historian are linked in that their hermeneutic awareness makes possible the interpretation of the relation of text and context.

Gadamer's position can be summarized by defining historiography as a kind of general philology (*WM* 322). This claim should not be confused, however, with a position that history is purely literary—at least in a traditionally *aesthetic* sense of the term as involving autonomous, unhistorical creation. The hermeneutic criticism of the aesthetic consciousness entails a corresponding revision of the ontological status of the literary artwork. When the term "literature" no longer designates written work in general (such as the "literature" on *Ulysses* or on DNA) but assigns the status of poetic art to a text, it is being used normatively rather than descriptively and thus presupposes a decision about a difference of degree between the ordinary and the poetic texts. From the aesthetic standpoint the difference is generally taken to be the *form* of the writing—that is, traditionally, the beauty of expression or, more recently, the structure of the writing. According to the hermeneutic account, however, what is said is as important as how it is said, and the essential difference between the two sorts of texts lies in the truth-*expectations* (Wahrheitsanspruch) of the texts (*WM* 155). The figurative language of literature does not yield the same clarity and distinctness as the more prosaic language of history. Yet this is not to say that literary language does not generate any expectation of truth. The pleasure of a dramatic production is, for Gadamer, a cognitive pleasure, although of a general sort—like, for instance, a self-recognition or the recognition of a true depiction of the human situation. Pure lyric is more problematic because it is essentially ambiguous—*vieldeutig*. Even ambiguity implies the recognition of meaning, however; it is not nonsense but indicates precisely the recognition of the many possible directions meaning can take. *Dichten* is also *Deuten*—poetizing is also a way of giving meaning, of signifying (see *KS* II 9 ff.). Language involves an essential movement of saying something about a subject matter. But the matter need not be external or extrinsic, and in the case of the poem, it can be the poetic language itself.

Understanding a text entails an understanding of the subject matter about which the text speaks, even if this subject is the nature of poetry itself. Furthermore, to understand the text and the reason for making the text the object of inquiry, there must be some reflection (more or less explicit) on the cognitive motivations behind the inquiry. Textual understanding therefore also involves a process of self-understanding: what must be understood are not only the words in the text and their relations, but also the reasons why the text exerts a claim on the reader—in this case precisely the claim of being poetry. The literary text is different from the historical *document*—and from the historical document into which Barthes's history of functions would transform the literary text—because the reader is the direct addressee of that text, which is thus a voice from the present (*KS* II 5). To suspend the movement toward meaning in the poetry, a movement toward saying something true about a subject matter (which can be, again, poetry itself) is to overlook the way poetry is constitutive of the cultural horizon in which the interpreter himself stands. The poetic text is not something *vergangenes,* completely past, but stands in the present as the *Überlieferung,* the tradition. The tradition, again, is not over and done with; it is still working itself out in the present. The poetry is part of that tradition, and as such its meaning for the self-understanding of the present cannot be ignored. The self-understanding at stake in the hermeneutic consciousness throughout the process of historical and literary interpretation is therefore not simply subjective but includes such dimensions as the methodological self-understanding of the discipline, the social role and force of the discipline, or even an interpretation of the present age as such. The blindness of the interpreter to these dimensions of his thought is not proof that they are not significant possibilities.

V. HERMENEUTICS AND PRACTICAL CRITICISM:
JAUSS, STAIGER, RIFFATERRE, FISH

As a philosophical theory of the nature of understanding and interpretation, Gadamer's hermeneutics does not entail any particular method of practical criticism, but it has nevertheless influenced literary critics who are concerned with questions of methodology. In fact, the most influential aspect of hermeneutical theory is its emphasis on influence, on the tradition of the reception of literary works as a constituent of the understanding of these works and of literature per se. Any theory of criticism emphasizing meaning and its reception rather than psychological intention and genesis has an affinity with the hermeneutical tradition of Heidegger and Gadamer. Some literary critics—for example, Emil Staiger and Hans Robert Jauss—are more directly influenced by this tradition, but others—such as the American critics Stanley Fish and Harold Bloom—also must be understood in its context. No single theorist of practical criticism represents the best expression of the spirit of hermeneutical philosophy, but it is instructive to review several theories that illustrate possible applications—or misapplications—of the central hermeneutical concept of *wirkungsgeschichtliches Bewusstsein* in a theory of literary history.

Hans Robert Jauss, a former student of Gadamer's and a scholar of French literature, develops the methodological notion of *Wirkungsgeschichte*—the history of interpretations and their interaction with other historical occurrences—into a specific philological method, and thus demonstrates some of the ramifications of this hermeneutic awareness. In the essay "Geschichte der Kunst und Historie," Jauss gives an illuminating analysis of the use of fictional narrative in Ranke's historiography, and shows how Ranke's writing is conditioned by an aesthetic paradigm (adopting the term "paradigm" from Thomas Kuhn) provided by a conceptual framework of aesthetic categories drawn from Winckelmann. Jauss's main thesis consists of showing that literary history need not be patterned on the paradigm of historiography. While literary history today may be dominated by the constraints of a positivistic understanding of the nature of scientific historiography, Jauss shows that earlier historiography—that of Droysen, for example— was modeled on the paradigm of the historical understanding of artworks. Of current literary history Jauss writes, "The scientifi- cally sanctioned form of literary history is the worst imaginable medium for catching sight of the historicity [Geschichtlichkeit] of literature."[7] Jauss suggests that literary history is not adequately described by comparison with positivist historiography and holds that historiography can itself benefit from being modeled on the paradigm of the history of art. In the course of the argument Jauss, obviously influenced by Gadamer and in agreement with the notion of the fusion of horizons (see p. 242n), nevertheless crit- icizes Gadamer's notion of tradition (see pp. 232, 235, 242, 249). Jauss, too, misunderstands the philosophical force of Gadamer's concept of tradition (as "Überlieferungs*geschehen*") and over- emphasizes its materialistic and substantialist component.

Jauss, however, is generally very close in spirit to Gadamer's theory. In the important essay "Literaturgeschichte als Provo- kation der Literaturwissenschaft" Jauss proposes a "rezeptions- geschichtliche Methode" (method of historical reception) that "not only pursues throughout history a poet's success, posthu- mous fame, and influence, but also investigates the historical con- ditions and modifications of his comprehension" (p. 183). Jauss insists even more strongly than Gadamer that interpretive under- standing involves not only a reproductive, but also a productive moment (p. 188; see also *WM* 280). He therefore develops his own hermeneutical aesthetic (Rezeptionsästhetik) as a framework in which to understand the foundations of literary history. This framework, he maintains,

must take the historicity of literature into consideration in three respects: dia- chronically in the context of the reception of literary works . . . ; synchronically in the system of relations of the contemporary literature and in the consequences of such systems . . . ; and finally in the relation of the immanent literary develop- ments to the general course of history.   [P. 189]

Jauss's theory thus follows Gadamer's in criticizing the objectivistic presuppositions of an aesthetic emphasizing production and representation (Produktions- und Darstellungsästhetik) and strives to develop the practical, philological consequences of an aesthetic emphasizing reception and influence (Rezeptions- und Wirkungsästhetik). Jauss transforms the hermeneutic insistence on the moment of self-understanding in interpretation into an explicit and radical normative principle:

The rank of a literary history founded in the aesthetic of reception will depend upon the extent to which it is able to participate actively in the continual totalizing [Totalisierung] of the past through aesthetic experience. That requires on the one hand—in contrast to the objectivism of positivistic literary history—a consciously aspired-to formulation of canons, and on the other—in contrast to the classicism of research into the tradition—a critical, if not even destructive, revision of the inherited and presupposed literary canons.   [P. 170]

Another example of the possible force of the hermeneutic awareness for practical criticism can be seen in a proposal by Emil Staiger that illustrates the important connections between strictly aesthetic questions and more historical questions. Staiger, who attempts "to evaluate a work of art artistically—in the strict sense of the word—rather than politically or morally or religiously," can nevertheless include hermeneutic-historical considerations among his aesthetic criteria. Thus, to the usual criteria for aesthetic goodness (such as unison, individuality, uniqueness of language, loyalty to literary species) Staiger adds such conditions as the *weight* of the literary work in the balance of history and the power to create a sense of *community* (that is, a sense of the age or of a tradition).[8] While all these criteria are in themselves debatable, the latter two, while historical, are not extraliterary.

These considerations are rather general, however, and other literary critics have developed more detailed methods of stylistic analysis in a theoretical framework which nevertheless emphasizes reception and response. Although Michael Riffaterre and Stanley Fish work out of entirely different traditions from Jauss and Gadamer, their concern for the process of reading as an essential determinant of the meaning of the literary text represents possible ways of spelling out the mechanics of reception and *Wirkungsgeschichte*.

Michael Riffaterre's well-known critique of the analysis of Baudelaire's "les Chats" by Jakobson and Lévi-Strauss shares the reservations of many literary scholars about the ability of structural linguistics to capture the "poetry" in a particular piece of language.[9] Riffaterre thinks that the structures picked out by the linguistic analysis are often not perceptible and cannot be the specific features generating the reader's empirical feeling that the text is a poem. In contrast to the linguistic "superpoem" constructed by Jakobson and Lévi-Strauss, Riffaterre builds a "superreader" based on the responses of a variety of readers.

The details of his stylistic analysis need not be described here, since the parallel to hermeneutical, reception theories lies in Riffaterre's insistence that the poem be seen as response. Riffaterre's superreader thus takes anything that holds up a reader and attracts his attention as an objective sign of the actuality of a contact with the poem, and as a clue to its poetic structure. This structure is understood in terms of binary oppositions that generate unpredictable contrasts ("DPS" 203-204).

Two features of this theory of the poem as response must be noted. First, there is an important sense in which Riffaterre is in agreement with the hermeneutical insistence that the *Sache* or subject matter be included in any account of the process of understanding poetry or literature. Contrary to the anticognitivist attempt by theorists such as I. A. Richards to dissociate literature from message, content, or information, Riffaterre's stylistics accommodates message as an essential part—although not the most important one—of the poetic phenomenon ("DPS" 202).

Second, however, there is also a sense in which Riffaterre's method remains closer to structuralism than to hermeneutics, for the superreader appears in this article to be curiously synchronic and unhistorical. All readings, regardless of time, place, and situation, are brought together to create one idealized act of reading. In fact, Riffaterre explicitly empties the response of its content (ideology, background, or purposes) and uses it only as a cue to the linguistic devices of the work ("DPS" 203). This synchrony is, of course, not necessarily a defect in his method of stylistic analysis, but it shows that the theory does not fully express the *wirkungsgeschichtliches Bewusstsein* that Gadamer thinks is essential to literary interpretation.

Stanley Fish, on the other hand, develops an alternative approach to stylistics that he claims is in fact radically historical. Also an accomplished literary historian, Fish defends what is probably the most radical version of response-oriented theory. In the seminal essay "Literature in the Reader: Affective Stylistics,"[10] he argues for the constitutive role of the reader, but in a way that will purportedly do justice to the "matrix of political, cultural, and literary determinants" behind each reading, and hence to "local conditions, [including] local notions of literary value" ("LR" 407-408). If successful, this program would link the concept of response with the more historical notions of reception and influence as developed by Jauss and others.

Like Hirsch's theory, Fish's takes much of its rhetorical point from its opposition to Wimsatt and Beardsley. Whereas Hirsch is preoccupied with the intentional fallacy, Fish attacks their companion essay, "The Affective Fallacy." This piece maintains that the psychological response of the reader is as extrinsic a source of evidence for the text's meaning as the author's intention:

> The Affective Fallacy is a confusion between the poem and its *results* (what it *is* and what it *does*), a special case of epistemological skepticism. . . . It begins by trying to derive the standard of criticism from the psychological effects of the poem and ends in impressionism and relativism. The outcome of either Fallacy, the Intentional or the Affective, is that the poem itself, as an object of specifically critical judgment, tends to disappear.[11]

Fish intends to demonstrate that the affective fallacy is itself fallacious by giving a different theory of meaning from that presupposed by Wimsatt and Beardsley. His basic point is well taken, for he maintains that response is not equivalent to affect, but includes complex cognitive operations in the process of understanding the words on a page. Rather than limit response to psychological feelings, Fish extends it to cover the total act of communication, and believes that the attempt to limit interpretation to the text as a thing-in-itself is overly abstract.

Instead of the New Critics' concern with the text, Fish offers "a method of analysis that focuses on the reader rather than on the artifact" ("LR" 400). His "affective stylistics" begins by asking what each word, sentence, paragraph, chapter, and so on, *does* (not what it *means*), and answers through "an analysis of the developing responses of the reader in relation to the words as they succeed one another in time" ("LR" 387-388). He is able to avoid the psychologism criticized by Wimsatt-Beardsley since his concept of response has nothing to do with "tears, prickles," and "other psychological symptoms,"[12] and his "reader," like Riffaterre's superreader, is a construct, not an actual living reader ("LR" 407).[13] This "informed reader" is really the set of all relevant syntactic and semantic competences, and is a linguistic ideal that the biographical critic should try to attain in order to give a reliable report of his experience of the literary work.

Fish's theory is thus akin to philosophical hermeneutics in its insistence that the literary work only comes to be in a process of understanding and interpretation. There are three important corollaries that follow from Fish's nonpsychologistic account of the linguisticality of the reading process. The first is concerned with the distinction between ordinary and poetic language, the second with the relevance of the message of the literary work as well as the *Sache* of literature as such, and the third with the status of intention.

Fish is convinced that the attempt to find specific linguistic features that distinguish poetry from other nonpoetic language is based on a misconception ("LR" 408). Rather than see poetry as a deviation from ordinary usage, and hence as abnormal or uniquely privileged, Fish sees ordinary language as involving the same sorts (although perhaps not the same degree) of complexity as poetic language. He thus attacks Riffaterre for setting up a separate method to deal with effects that are specifically poetic ("LR" 418). Of course, there must be some differences, even if only of degree and not of kind. Thus, on Fish's own account, literature is the *self-conscious* use of the resources of ordinary language, and it must be approached with different attitudes and expectations.

More germane to the present discussion is the second corollary, which follows from the first. For Fish, as for Riffaterre, the message is an important control on the reader's response, and is thus not to be excluded as irrelevant, as it would be in formalist criticism ("LR" 424-425). Again, the message is of course not necessarily the most important feature of a literary work, but literature is not to be distinguished from nonliterary language on the grounds that it is not message-bearing. Of course, as the self-conscious use of the resources of language, the poem's message could be a self-referential pointing to its own operations. Furthermore, message involves form as well as discursive doctrine, and Fish objects to emotivists like Richards who maintain that logic and argument are irrelevant to poetry. While coherence may be less important for some poetry and prose, Fish points out that cognitive processes, like calculating, comparing, deducing, are often essentially involved, as his own specialty, seventeenth-century literature, illustrates ("LR" 413-414). In hermeneutical terms, Fish's point is that the activity of understanding and interpretation is misconceived by the aesthetic reduction of literature to fiction and the disregard for its *Sache.*

A third corollary of such an emphasis on the reader concerns the relevance of the author's intention. Fish does not discuss the matter of intention in "Literature in the Reader," and in "Describing Poetic Structures" Riffaterre excludes it from consideration on the weak grounds that the poet is no longer present and that our knowledge of the author's intention, since historically derived, is external to the message ("DPS" 202). With the emphasis on the constitutive force of response, reading, and reception, however, the concept of the author's intention can also be seen in a new light. The argument in chapter one against probing the author's intention is directed specifically against psychologism. It goes beyond Wimsatt and Beardsley's "The Intentional Fallacy" in claiming that the author's intention must be rejected not only as a *standard,* but also as a *cause.* The purpose of the argument is to undercut the traditional priority given to such a concept. On the other hand, the argument does not altogether exclude the author's expressed intention—his own reflection on and interpretation of his work—for that interpretation may contain valid insights. The author's self-interpretation is as relevant as any other interpretation—although not necessarily more so. Its possible privilege comes from its place in and influence on the history of the work's interpretation. The author is another reader and as such must be respected. It does not follow, however, that respecting another's interpretation prohibits contesting it. (A similar argument applies to the interpretation represented by the work's reception by its original audience.)

While Fish's theory is useful in showing the narrowness of some

formalist tenets of criticism and the potential advantages of response theory, his own arguments sometimes commit him to paradoxical claims. His central argument against Wimsatt-Beardsley is
to be understood as a direct contradiction of their separation of
the meaning of a sentence from what it does. Saying of a particular
sentence that "what it does is what it means," Fish suggests that
"there is no direct relationship between the meaning of a sentence
(paragraph, novel, poem) and what its words mean" ("LR" 393).
A corollary of his view of meaning is that "it is impossible to mean
the same thing in two (or more) different ways" ("LR" 393).
Although his theory as explained in this article should depend on a
cogent alternative theory of meaning, his use of the term "meaning" is ambiguous and paradoxical. His specification that the
meaning of an utterance is the *experience* of the utterance does not
take him in the apparently desired direction of a speech act analysis of meaning but commits him to a pre-Wittgensteinian philosophy of mind, as does his claim that "the place where sense is made
or not made is the reader's mind rather than the printed page or
the space between the covers of a book" ("LR" 397). Since the
reader in question here is apparently the informed reader—not a
living person, but a linguistic construct—the term "experience"
appears to be figurative and unnecessary.

Fish thus risks the same difficulties that are shown in chapter
one to confront Hirsch in his appeal to a psychological experience
that is independent of its linguistic expression. What has happened, apparently, is that the rejection of the author's intention
and genetic criticism is perceived as leaving one with a choice between the printed page or the reader's mind as the locus of "meaning." Wimsatt-Beardsley choose the former, and Fish the latter.
But Fish's view is much more subtle than this, and it is possible
that his theory of meaning could be worked out in terms of post-
Wittgensteinian speech act theorists like Austin and Searle. This
would be a difficult task, however, and could only be debated
when completed. Short of such a theory, one is inclined to believe
that Fish is not really talking about meaning in a univocal way, but
slides between what chapter one called "sense" and "significance."

Fish himself does not intend to talk about significance in the
sense of "doctrine" or "value," however, When his method is

applied, he insists that "it refuses to answer or even ask the question, what is this work about" ("LR" 399). It avoids ever "coming to the point" of the literary work, since "coming to the point is the goal of a criticism that believes in content, in extractable meaning" ("LR" 410). Why this almost formalist abstention from consideration of the message should be necessary is unclear, however, given his other argument that the message is at least part of the response to the work. This abstention, plus the fact that Fish's method admittedly makes it difficult to say that "one work is better than another or even that a single work is good or bad" ("LR" 408), may appear to confirm the feeling behind "The Affective Fallacy" that response-oriented criticism ends in relativism. Fish's only response is the rather unlikely claim that readings do not differ in response at the level of the *description* of works, but only at the level of their *evaluation* ("LR" 409-410). More revealing of his difficulty is his own claim to prefer "an acknowledged and controlled subjectivity" to an illusory objectivity.

The objectivity Fish has in mind, of course, is the result of the decision to limit criticism to the text itself, the "object of specifically critical judgment" that "The Affective Fallacy" thinks "tends to disappear" in response-oriented criticism. The objectivity of the text is only an illusion for Fish since what is really to be described is the process of reading. In this process the poem is not a given, static object, but is constantly changing—"and therefore no 'object' at all" ("LR" 401).

At this point, Fish takes the notion of response so far that the text has indeed entirely disappeared into the reader's context. Yet a response theory or reception theory that has nothing to respond to or to receive is indeed paradoxical.[14] While the text may not be an independently given thing-in-itself, there is no need to infer that it is nothing, or that it does not exist. For instance, if the message is granted to be a dimension of the reading process, then to infer that a poem is about love when it is about death is to make a mistake about the text. Wrong message, wrong poem. Of course, the text may be structured so as to elicit "wrong" responses in order to heighten the desired response. As the result of an analysis of *The Pilgrim's Progress,* Fish himself concludes that the result of his method will be "a description of the structure of response which may have an oblique or even . . . a contrasting relationship to the structure of the work as a thing-in-itself" ("LR" 399). But if the response is a relation, as Fish himself admits, then there must be another term, the thing responded to, in the relation. Fish's remark indicates that he has not really freed himself from the concept of the "thing-in-itself" altogether, and indeed, his paradox, like Nietzsche's, results from holding on to notions— such as the reader's "mind" and the textual "thing-in-itself," and perhaps even the notion of psychological "response" or "experience"—which on his own terms should be abandoned.

Apart from these difficulties, Fish's emphasis on the linguisticality (not the psychology) of the reading process, and his approach to stylistics are valuable contributions to the development of a reception theory of literary criticism. A hermeneutical philosophy need not accept, of course, the particular programs of reception theorists like Jauss, Riffaterre, or Fish, but their point is well taken that literary history must be freed from the objectivistic illusions of both purely aesthetic and purely historical consciousness. It is not the task of literary history to reconstruct what appeared before the author as he wrote the text. According to the hermeneutic accounts of both Gadamer and Jauss, such a reductive construal of literary history overlooks the essential point that all literary interpretation is in an important sense literary history. The act of interpretation itself generates the history of the literary text, and literature is essentially historical in that the work does not exist independently of the tradition of interpretations in which it is understood.

VI. THE PARADOX OF MODERNITY: HAROLD BLOOM

The Nietzschean antinomy between poetry and history is problematic not only for the literary historian but also for the poet or other literary creator. Both literature and literary history present us with the problem of understanding how something can both inhere in a tradition—and hence be historical—and yet contain, or attain, a unique originality that transcends the tradition. Given the hermeneutic thesis of the continuity of history and tradition, how could a discontinuity, a genuinely creative poetic act, occur? How can the new emerge?

The hermeneutic notion of *Wirkungsgeschichte* and the emphasis on the authority and continuity of tradition do not, in Gadamer's opinion, preclude the possibility of original creativity. Again, to think that the *wirkungsgeschichtliches Bewusstsein* would prohibit the appearance of the new or revolutionary is to misunderstand the concept. History is misconceived by the common picture of it as an organic continuity that develops independently without interruption. For Gadamer, on the contrary, the tradition does not evolve with that kind of certainty, and it does not have "the innocence of organic life." Rather, it can be "resisted with revolutionary fervor when . . . found to be lifeless and inflexible" (*KS* I 160).

The point could be amplified by noting that literature tends to depend upon a tradition for its place and its possibilities and that this tradition perhaps demands internal revolution. It may be *essential* to do something that has not been done before. An author deliberately trying to do something that *has* been done before would still be trying to do something different, something new, something that his contemporaries who are all trying to be "original" are not doing. Much of what is written, however, fails to do anything new, possibly because the reflection upon what has been done before has not been pushed far enough.

Of course, for hermeneutical philosophy to argue that aesthetic novelty is not precluded does not make the task of the poet any easier. That there is no epistemological paradox involved in the philosophical position does not mean that the poet will have fewer difficulties in finding his own voice. The hermeneutical theory thus dissolves only the philosophical paradoxes associated with historicism. It does not dissolve the historicist insight that what counts as poetry, or even as philosophy, is subject to change. In fact, the most essential task of the poet, the critic, and perhaps the philosopher may be to contribute to change in their own disciplines.

One literary critic who shares the historicist intuitions behind hermeneutical philosophy and embeds them in a rich theory of literary history is Harold Bloom. His book, *The Anxiety of Influence*,[15] is both more and less than the "theory of poetry" promised in the subtitle, for it projects a theory of our culture and of modernity as such. Because the academic philosopher has withdrawn from the cultural "Scene of Instruction," the literary critic steps in to supply a diagnosis of the modern mind's attempt to think creatively at the same time that it reflects on its own genesis and historical condition.

Bloom's book is a theory of literary history that goes beyond a concern for how the interpreter deals with the literary object (although it comes back to that) and considers the historical self-awareness—one could say the *wirkungsgeschichtliches Bewusstsein*—of the poet. Strictly speaking, Bloom is also dealing with the hermeneutical awareness of the poetry itself, for his poet is the "poet in a poet" (*AI* 11), not the biographical person. The meaning of a poem, according to Bloom's theory of poetic influence, is a function of the reading, but a reading that leads not to the reduction of the poem to "something that is not itself a poem" but to *"another poem"* (*AI* 70), a precursor poem.

Bloom's theory of literary history is thus strictly immanent or intrinsic to poetry as such, and poetry is not to be explained by reducing it to extrinsic factors such as "images, ideas, given things, or phonemes" (*AI* 94). At the same time, Bloom's theory accounts for poetic history because it interprets poems diachronically through other poems. As a theory of interpretation it would thus avoid paradox because it recognizes both that poetry must be regarded as immanent and that this immanence does not prescind historicity. The poem stands in relation to a tradition of poetry, a tradition that need not be fully conscious to be operant. Bloom takes over the Freudian idea of tradition as "equivalent to repressed material in the mental life of the individual" (*AI* 109). He can thus make the surprising claim that the precursor poem need not even be one that the disciple poet—the ephebe—has ever read (*AI* 70). Influence is not something that can be escaped, whether through innocence or ignorance. No imagination is possible without influence (*AI* 154), and Bloom believes that even the great modern deniers of influence, such as Goethe, Nietzsche, Mann, Blake, Rousseau, and Hugo, ironically manifest a deep anxiety of influence (*AI* 56). Nor can precursors be simply forgotten, for forgetting, as Nietzsche also recognizes, is a willed process of repression, not of liberation: "Every forgotten precursor," says Bloom, "becomes a giant of the imagination" (*AI* 107).

If a poem thus represents a reading of a precursor poem, whether or not an actual reading takes place, the reading must be of a special sort. It must prevent the influence of the precursor from overwhelming and subsuming the new poem: "Every good reader properly *desires* to drown, but if the poet drowns, he will become *only a reader*" (*AI* 57). Influence is the essential anxiety of the modern mind as it faces the tension in the precursor's demand to "be me but not me" (*AI* 70). The ephebe's reading of the precursor must be a misreading or misinterpretation: "If the ephebe is to avoid over-determination, he needs to forsake correct perception of the poems he values most" (*AI* 71).

The history of poetry since Shakespeare, on Bloom's theory, is a "map of misreadings," and the common denominator of these misreadings—the hidden subject of poetry—is the anxiety of influence (*AI* 152). Two admitted influences behind Bloom's poetical theory are Freud and Nietzsche. Freud supplies the metaphors of motivation, Nietzsche the rhetoric of paradox and power. Modern poetry is for Bloom a family romance, with the ephebe struggling against the anxiety caused by the strength and authority of the father-figure, the precursor poet (sometimes a composite figure) who appears to be the last, unsurpassable monument in the history of poetry. The ephebe thirsts for discontinuity, for a break or swerve in this history that will allow him to displace his precursor and stand in his stead—just as the child who learns he owes life to his parents wants to repay the father (perhaps by saving his life) but also wishes to repay the mother (by becoming the father himself).[16]

What the ephebe desires his creation to be is really a reorganization of the history of poetry, with himself as its culmination. This reorganization should be so complete, however, that the normal sequence of influence is reversed. Instead of the usual forward causation whereby an earlier poet is seen as influencing a later one, Bloom's theory suggests a backward causation. The particular passages of the precursor's work are not to be seen merely as presages of the later poet's advent; rather, the precursor is to appear indebted to (and lessened by) the achievement and splendor of the later poet (*AI* 141). The strong poet is the one who succeeds in making us see the earlier work in a way that we could not have without his appearance, for it is "as though the later poet himself had written the precursor's characteristic work" (*AI* 16). Bloom thus finds that truer than Kierkegaard's statement that "he who is willing to work gives birth to his own father" is Nietzsche's aphorism, "When one hasn't had a good father, it is necessary to invent one" (*AI* 56).

Bloom is indeed fully cognizant of the paradox of modernity described by Nietzsche. Unlike Nietzsche, but for different reasons from de Man's, Bloom rejects the solution of appealing to youth as a way of transcending the sickness of historical, reflective consciousness. Although youth may think they are pure, they are not. One is inevitably involved in history, and in a savage, perverse, swerving relation to it (*AI* 85). Bloom is also aware that the difficulty faced by the creative poet is not merely a conceptual one, but is built into the very enterprise of poetry. The conceptual puzzle of how literary history can make sense of both poetic influence and poetic originality is easily put aside with the casual but true remark that "poetic influence need not make poets less original; as often it makes them more original, though not therefore necessarily better" (*AI* 7).

Bloom can dissolve the paradox of influence and novelty precisely because he is advancing a form of reception theory, one that emphasizes the reading of poetry and the cumulative feedback of the tradition in determining the understanding of poetic works. On the surface, Bloom is dispelling the myth of an innocent, unmotivated writing of poetry by pointing to the jealousy and anxiety behind the writing, making it a deliberate misreading (*AI* 86). At another level, however, to see that Bloom is a reception theorist is to recognize that what looks like a psychology of the "poet in a poet" is actually a recommendation to the good reader, the literary critic. In fact, Bloom's theory cannot really be a theory of poetry. All it says about poetry is that what counts as poetry is subject to change. The theory is historicist in the sense that it makes poetry relative to paradigms generated at different times by whoever becomes the next strong poet. No standards are given for what counts as poetry, and in fact none can be given, for the anxiety of influence underlying all poetry is indeterminate in itself and relative to its particular historical situation.

As a theory not of poetry but of criticism, however, a curious displacement of the poet and of poetics occurs. Since the success of the poetic will-to-power depends upon generating a new vision of the history of poetry, who is better equipped than the literary historian-critic to carry out this task? Strong poets may eventually give way to strong critics, and indeed the distinction is already difficult to discern. Bloom himself calls his book a "severe poem" (*AI* 13), and argues that criticism and poetry are only dissimilar in degree. The current difference is simply that the critic has more parents since his precursors are both poets and critics (*AI* 95). Bloom calls for an antithetical criticism that sees poems as antithetical misreadings of other poems. Yet since the meaning of a poem is only another poem, and poems are misreadings, he draws the consequence that "there are no interpretations but only misinterpretations, and so all criticism is prose poetry" (*AI* 95).

The difficulty with this theory of criticism is that just as there are no determinate standards for poetry, so are there no criteria for criticism. Or perhaps the only criterion is success. On this issue, however, Bloom appears to fall back into Nietzsche's paradox. He even borrows Nietzsche's paradoxical language and says:

The issue is true history or rather the true use of it, rather than the abuse of it, both in Nietzsche's sense. True poetic history is the story of how poets as poets have suffered other poets.   [*AI* 94]

Since "truth" here is a matter of use or purpose, it is not clear whether a "true" poetic history would be based on anything more than a critic's ability to persuade other critics that his account is more interesting than other accounts. The purpose of literary history for Bloom (although not for Nietzsche) might thus be only the critic's own ego-gratification. Such a subjectivism, however, would clearly undercut the very activity of criticism. For if every critic really believed that his own and others' understandings of literary history were arbitrary, and that their activity was only the exertion of will-to-power in the effort to be the next strong critic, there would be no basis for even the minimal amount of required consensus. Something more is necessary to explain how one critic can have a better argument or a more penetrating vision than another.

Of course, Bloom's own vision of modern culture is essentially entropic, and he might not shirk this nihilistic result. Anxiety is essentially about death, and since Bloom is not discussing the biographical person but the poet in a poet, the anxiety of influence is also an anxiety about the death of poetry. The situation of culture today is like that of poetry, and Bloom's picture of poetry is rather like Nietzsche's sense of the emergent nihilism of recent times. If poetry after Shakespeare begins looking back over its shoulder, gradually, in the nineteenth and twentieth centuries, it becomes obsessed with itself and with its awareness of its constant backward glance. Post-Enlightenment poetry may always have been poetry about poetry. When it becomes conscious of being only this, however, it may not be able, following Nietzsche's analysis in the *Genealogy of Morals,* to escape the nihilistic recognition that it only reflects a blind and empty will-to-nothingness.

The death of poetry may itself be promoted by the rise of criticism, for as one Bloom reviewer puts it, "the newest thin volumes seem completely transparent, thanks to the powerful beams instantly focused upon them from a thousand critical angles."[17] But if poetry ceases, can the death of criticism be far behind? Freeing criticism from its object may open it up to all the possibilities of rich imaginations; yet if it sees itself only as imagination and not as knowledge (for there is now no truth of the matter), then nothing keeps it too from succumbing to the sickness of the modern imagination's obsessive self-consciousness. When the critic like the poet realizes the point is to become the next strong critic, then a sheer struggle for power ensues, and criticism becomes not latent but blatant aggression. For the will-to-power to make itself evident as what it is, however, is to defeat its own purpose. Criticism thus becomes pointless if the reading is the result of merely an arbitrary imagination, however rich.

From a hermeneutical perspective, then, Bloom's theory has the advantage of showing that the project of literary history can be construed in such a way that the demands of aesthetic consciousness are reconciled with those of a historicist one. Within the hermeneutic circle there is no unbridgeable tension between poetry and history, since poetry comes to be through an interpretive understanding that is essentially historical. Yet despite this valid recognition of the historicity of poetry, Bloom's theory fails to overcome the danger of nihilism that lurks behind Nietzsche's own inadequate understanding of the historical consciousness. Gadamer's hermeneutical theory goes beyond Nietzsche by giving a different description of the phenomenon of the fusion of horizons in the *wirkungsgeschichtliches Bewusstsein.* This fusion is effected through the mediation of the *Sache,* or subject matter, which underlies *both* the past and the present horizons. Bloom's slip back into nihilism thus evolves from his lack of an account of the *Sache* of poetry itself and hence an inability to speak about the truth-expectations of both poetry and criticism. Whether his theory could ultimately fill in this lack is an open question—one that may be most critical for any future poetics. Gadamer's hermeneutical philosophy does not itself provide such a normative poetics. Its value is rather that it specifies the elements that must be included in any process of human understanding. While current reception theories illustrate how these elements may be applied, in some instances they thus also illustrate the problems that result from ignoring particular elements and closing the hermeneutic circle too quickly.

VII. LITERARY HISTORY AND THE INTERPRETIVE CIRCLE: A SYNOPSIS

The hermeneutical analysis of the interrelation of literary understanding and historical understanding follows from and encapsulates the arguments of previous chapters for the essential interconnection of understanding, interpretation, and criticism. Poetic truth is interpretive truth in the sense that the work has to be brought into an interpretation even to be understood. This movement raises the danger of relativism, the possibility that anything at all can be read into the text. Therefore criticism of the interpretation and its validity and legitimacy must be possible. But criticism is possible only if the understanding of the text is interpretive (if the one right understanding of the text were immediately given, criticism of the understanding would not be necessary or even possible). To understand how the text has been interpreted, the understanding that conditioned the interpretation must be examined; understanding of the text is also self-understanding. But such self-understanding is always interpretive, since one can never completely objectify oneself.

One corollary is that just as understanding is self-understanding, criticism must also imply self-criticism.[18] Criticism of another interpretation itself involves an interpretation. Since this interpretation is itself merely interpretive, self-criticism is in order—even if the critic is not able to specify his own blindness, and even if he believes that all interpretation involves both blindness and insight.

Another corollary states that interpretation is essentially a historical process, the result of the critical interaction of a community of discourse. Hence the reaction of others to the interpretation is an important test of its value. Furthermore, if the interpretation moves toward methodical self-reflection, if criticism is not dogmatic but self-conscious, this consciousness will necessarily include the *wirkungsgeschichtliches Bewusstsein*—the hermeneutic awareness of the tradition of interpretation influencing present understanding.

Interpretation thus involves a self-interpretation of the tradition of a work's reception. New interpretations have critical force insofar as they continue a dialogue with the text and demonstrate the limitations of previous explorations of the text. This implicit or explicit act of criticism of the tradition does not, however, necessarily represent a complete break with it. Criticism of the tradition can also be a way of connecting with the tradition, of showing the truth of the tradition by revealing the falseness of what the present mistakenly takes to be "traditional." A poem continues to have an effect as long as the dialogue leads to greater self-awareness of current questions and methodologies. As self-awareness increases, consequences become clearer and the need for subsequent self-criticism becomes evident. The literary-historical aspect of literary interpretation, then, is not only the moment when the interpreter attempts to step back into the poem's past. Literary history also involves an essential relation to the present by producing self-awareness and self-criticism. Reflection on the partiality of past interpretations demands reflection on the partiality of the present.

The analysis of literary history which made the very project of literary history seem paradoxical is therefore based on an illusion. The idea of past and present as alienated spheres, closed to each other, is misguided. The historical consciousness of the differences between past and present contains implicitly the hermeneutic awareness that the present is conditioned by the past insofar as the present stands in a tradition that includes the past. Literary history is not paradoxical if one remembers that to understand history is to try to understand the present (revealed in the fact that the text is "literary"), and to understand the present, one has to understand the work's and one's own participation in a tradition (hence, the "historicity" of the literary). The immanence of the literary text is itself historical insofar as the text is capable of being transcendent or transhistorical. To call the text transhistorical is not to imply, with a purely aesthetic stance, that the text embodies some context-free, eternal meaning. Rather, it implies that the text has meaning only because it appears to a particular historical generation to be *literature*—that is, to assert a claim on that generation, to be "contemporary for every present" (*WM* 115). Such a claim is manifested precisely in that the text is granted the status of immanence. The relation is circular but that should not be surprising. There have always been works that have withstood the tooth of time and remained great over the ages. Although the status of a "classic" does not guarantee resistance to time, it may increase the probability of such resistance. The claim to immanence tends to be self-fulfilling.

Although hermeneutical philosophy is a theory of praxis, it is still a philosophical theory and cannot guarantee the methods of practical literary criticism, including the attribution of immanence to particular works. On the other hand, it does ascribe a paradigmatic importance to the encounter with literature. Literary interpretation is not simply one humanistic discipline among others, but brings the essential operations of these disciplines together in a way that heightens and focuses methodological difficulties. The successful resolution of these difficulties at the level of hermeneutical philosophy—and the extension of such methodological solutions to other branches of the humanities—would not eliminate the need for new interpretations. Since these interpretations reflect the successive self-understanding of generations and cultures, there will always be a need for the investigation both of new analytic methods and of old cultural foundations.

Nor does hermeneutical philosophy itself escape this worldly turmoil through the retreat to tranquil contemplation. Although it is only beginning to be recognized as a distinctive research program in twentieth-century philosophy, the previous chapters show that there are already conflicts and debates about its principles and goals. These tensions should not be interpreted, however, as a sign of despair or decline. Only the confrontation with further questions and problems will assure us of the vitality and viability of philosophical hermeneutics.

Notes

Introduction

1. See Paul Ricoeur, *De l'interprétation: essai sur Freud* (Paris: Seuil, 1965), now available in translation from Northwestern University Press. See also Hans-Georg Gadamer, "Hermeneutik als praktische Philosophie," in *Zur Rehabilitierung der praktischen Philosophie,* Vol. I, ed. M. Riedel (Freiburg: Verlag Rombach, 1972), pp. 334 f.

2. Martin Heidegger, *Being and Time,* trans. J. Macquarrie and E. Robinson (New York: Harper & Row, 1962), p. 62 (*SZ* 37); pages will also be cited from the original German text of *Sein und Zeit* (hereafter cited as *SZ*).

3. P. F. Strawson has advanced a similar argument about philosophy itself in his article: "Different Conceptions of Analytical Philosophy," *Tijdschrift voor Filosofie,* 35, 4 (December 1973), 800-834, see p. 816.

4. For further discussion see David Couzens Hoy, "History, Historicity, and Historiography in *Being and Time,*" in *Heidegger and Modern Philosophy: Critical Essays,* ed. Michael Murray (New Haven: Yale University Press, 1978); also, "The Owl and the Poet: Heidegger's Critique of Hegel," *Boundary 2,* 4 (1976), 393-410.

5. Hans-Georg Gadamer, *Wahrheit und Methods: Grundzüge einer philosophischen Hermeneutik,* 3d ed. (Tübingen: J. C. B. Mohr, 1975) (hereafter cited directly from the German as *WM,* since the recent English translation from Seabury Press uses other terms for some key concepts). Gadamer's collected essays are cited from the several volume *Kleine Schriften* (Tubingen: J. C. B. Mohr, 1967) (hereafter cited as *KS*). Some of these essays are available in English in *Philosophical Hermeneutics,* trans. David E. Linge (Berkeley, Los Angeles, London: University of California Press, 1976), and *Hegel's Dialectic: Five Hermeneutical Studies,* trans. P. Christopher Smith (New Haven: Yale University Press, 1976).

6. E. D. Hirsch, Jr., *Validity in Interpretation* (New Haven: Yale University Press, 1967).

7. See E. D. Hirsch, Jr., *The Aims of Interpretation* (Chicago: The University of Chicago Press, 1976), pp. 4 f., as well as chapts. two and five. See also Emilio Betti, *Die Hermeneutik als allgemeine Methodik der Geisteswissenschaften* (Tübingen: J. C. B. Mohr, 1962) (hereafter cited as *HMG*).

8. Geoffrey Hartman, *Beyond Formalism: Literary Essays, 1958-1970* (New Haven: Yale University Press, 1970), p. 42. Paul de Man, "Impasse de la critique formaliste," *Critique,* 12 (1956), 483-500; p. 489. See also de Man, "The Crisis of Contemporary Criticism," *Arion,* 6, 1 (Spring 1967); and "Literary History and Literary Modernity," *Daedelus* (Spring 1970), reprinted in *Blindness and Insight: Essays in the Rhetoric of Contemporary Criticism* (New York: Oxford University Press, 1971).

One: Validity and the Author's Intention

1. Wilhelm Dilthey, *Gesammelte Schriften,* Vol. VII (Leipzig and Berlin, 1927), cf. H.-G. Gadamer, *Wahrheit und Methode,* p. 209; also Wolfhart Pannenberg, "Hermeneutics and Universal History," in *History and Hermeneutic* (New York: Harper & Row, 1967), p. 129.

2. See E. D. Hirsch, Jr., *Validity in Interpretation* (New Haven: Yale University Press, 1967), p. 242 (hereafter cited as *VI*).

3. Ibid. This quotation comes from an earlier essay attached as an appendix to the later book *Validity in Interpretation.* In the book itself Hirsch states that he no longer wants to speak of the verification of interpretations, but only of validation: "To verify is to show that a conclusion is true; to validate is to show that a conclusion is probably true on the basis of what is known" (*VI* 171). Difficulties with this distinction will also be shown in section II of this chapter.

4. The term *words,* Hirsch admits, is used only approximately, to mean not individual words but "larger, sentence-like groupings of words" (*VI* 85 n. 10).

5. See Gilbert Harman, *Thought* (Princeton: Princeton University Press, 1973), p. 109.

6. W. V. Quine, *Words and Objections,* ed. D. Davidson and J. Hintikka (Dordrecht: Reidel, 1969), p. 306. See also Richard Rorty, "Indeterminacy of Translation and of Truth," *Synthese* 23 (1972), 448, and 461 n. 20.

7. See Rorty, "Indeterminacy."

8. Gottlob Frege, "Logik," *Schriften zur Logik und Sprachphilosophie, Aus dem Nachlass,* ed. Gottfried Gabriel (Hamburg: Felix Meiner Verlag, 1971), p. 49.

9. Frege, "Über Sinn und Bedeutung," *Kleine Schriften,* ed. Ignacio Angelelli (Darmstadt: Wissenschaftliche Buchgesellschaft, 1967), pp. 148-149 (orig. pp. 32-33). See also *Schriften zur Logik und Sprachphilosophie, Aus dem Nachlass* for comments on *Dichtung,* pp. 25, 32, 40-49, 84-89, 137-138.

10. Frege, "Ausführungen über Sinn und Bedeutung," *Nachlass,* p. 32.

11. Frege, "Logik," *Nachlass,* pp. 46-48.

12. W. K. Wimsatt, Jr. and Monroe Beardsley, "The Intentional Fallacy," in W. K. Wimsatt, Jr., *The Verbal Icon: Studies in the Meaning of Poetry* (New York: Noonday Press, 1954, 1966) (hereafter cited as *Verbal Icon*). For Wimsatt's own reevaluation of the fallacy see his essay "Genesis: A Fallacy Revisited," in *The Disciplines of Criticism: Essays in Literary Theory, Interpretation, and History,* ed. Peter Demetz et al. (New Haven: Yale University Press, 1968). Although this essay mentions some of Hirsch's work, it was completed before the appearance of *Validity in Interpretation*. Wimsatt reaffirms his conclusion that "the intention of a literary artist qua intention is neither a valid ground for arguing the presence of a quality or a meaning in a given instance of his literary work nor a valid criterion for judging the value of that work" (p. 195). Monroe Beardsley has replied directly to Hirsch's *Validity in Interpretation*. In the essay "Textual Meaning and Authorial Meaning," which appears as part of a symposium on Hirsch's book published in *Genre* (1, no. 3), Beardsley also finds "something odd about the notion of 'willing' a meaning" and argues succinctly and precisely the consequences of his position that "texts acquire determinate meaning through the interactions of their words without the intervention of an authorial will" (p. 172).

13. *Verbal Icon,* p. 3. In "Genesis: A Fallacy Revisited" Wimsatt distinguishes understanding and evaluation more clearly, and rewrites this sentence accordingly: "The design or intention of the author is neither available nor desirable as a standard for judging *either the meaning or the value* of a work of literary art" (p. 222, emphases added).

14. Ludwig Wittgenstein, *Philosophical Investigations* (New York: Macmillan, 1965), par. 416, p. 125 (hereafter cited as *PI*).

15. R. Rhees, "Can There Be a Private Language?" in *Wittgenstein: The Philosophical Investigations,* ed. George Pitcher (Garden City, N.Y.: Doubleday, 1966), p. 275.

Two: The Nature of Understanding

1. *Generation* is a term used by both Dilthey and Heidegger; cf. Heidegger, *SZ* 385.

2. Cf. Karl Popper, *The Open Society and Its Enemies* (London: Routledge & Kegan Paul, 1957); for discussion of methodological individualism see, for instance, the articles by Maurice Mandelbaum and J. W. N. Watkins in *Theories of History,* ed. Patrick Gardiner (New York: Free Press, 1959).

3. *WM* 285. This self-reflection and self-consciousness is part of the phenomenon Gadamer calls "das wirkungsgeschichtliche Bewusstsein." This concept will be discussed at length.

4. H.-G. Gadamer, "Hermeneutik als praktische Philosophie," in *Zur Rehabilitierung der praktische Philosophie,* Vol. I, ed. M. Riedel (Freiburg: Verlag Rombach, 1972), p. 335.

5. Cf. Martin Heidegger, *Schellings Abhandlung Über das Wesen der menschlichen Freiheit (1809)* (Tübingen: Max Niemeyer, 1971), p. 13.

6. See Paul Ricoeur, *De l'interprétation: essai sur Freud;* also, Jürgen Habermas, *Erkenntnis und Interesse* (Frankfurt: Suhrkamp, 1968), chap. 10; available in English translation by Jeremy J. Shapiro from Beacon Press, 1971.

7. Cf. Jürgen Habermas, "Erkenntnis und Interesse," in *Technik und Wissenschaft als 'Ideologie'* (Frankfurt: Suhrkamp, 1973); for Gadamer's critique of the objectivity of the natural sciences and his discussion of the interests behind scientific knowing, see *WM* 427-432.

8. Cf. Gilbert Harman, *Thought* (Princeton: Princeton University Press, 1973), p. 157.

9. Gadamer, "Hermeneutik als praktische Philosophie," p. 326; see also *WM* 295 ff.

10. Gadamer, "Hermeneutik als praktische Philosophie," p. 323; citing Aristotle, *Politics* 1325b 21 ff.; see also *WM* 430-431 where Gadamer points out that the modern notion of theory is largely privative, defining the absence or secondariness of any practical applicability of knowledge (as when a natural scientist acquires new knowledge for its own sake, without necessarily thinking about its possible uses).

11. Gadamer, "Hermeneutik als praktische Philosophie," p. 329, 343.

12. *Nicomachean Ethics* 1142a 24; all quotation are from the Ross translation.

13. For Gadamer, *Erfahrung* always entails a fundamental negativity. "To learn from experience" generally means to learn from a negative result. It can be objected that there are positive experiences, and the English term "experience" would certainly allow this. In German, however, there is a distinction between *Erfahrung* and *Erlebnis,* both of which translate as "experience." Gadamer analyzes the latter term as usually implying a unique, nonrepeatable, and often ineffable "experience," while the former is repeatable and alone allows for practical learning.

14. Charles Stevenson has advanced similar arguments in his essay "Relativism and Nonrelativism in the Theory of Value," in *Facts and Values* (New Haven: Yale University Press, 1963). This essay gives a clearer account of reasons than an earlier essay entitled "Interpretation and Evaluation in Aesthetics" (in *Philosophical Analysis,* ed. Max Black [Ithaca: Cornell University Press, 1950]), where Stevenson does turn the problem into a question of "individual differences" (p. 365).

Three: Text and Context

1. "Indem sich nämlich der Dichter mit dem reinen Ton seiner ursprünglichen Empfindung in seinem ganzen inneren und äusseren Leben begriffen fühlt und sich umsieht in seiner Welt, ist ihm diese ebenso neu und unbekannt, die Summe aller seiner Erfahrungen, seines Wissens, seines Anschauens, seines Gedenkens, Kunst und Natur, wie sie in ihm und ausser ihm sich darstellt, alles ist wie zum erstenmale, eben deswegen unbegriffen, unbestimmt, in lauter Stoff und Leben aufgelöst, ihm gegenwärtig. Und es ist vorzüglich wichtig, dass er in diesem

Augenblicke nichts als gegeben annehme, von nichts Positivem ausgehe, dass die Natur and Kunst, so wie er sie früher gelernt hat und sieht, nicht eher *spreche,* ehe für *ihn* eine Sprache da ist" (quoted by Gadamer, *WM* 445-446).

2. Jacques Derrida, "Differance," in *Speech and Phenomena, and Other Essays on Husserl's Theory of Signs,* trans. David B. Allison (Evanston: Northwestern University Press, 1973), p. 154 (hereafter cited as *SP*).

3. Jacques Derrida, *De la grammatologie* (Paris: Les Éditions de Minuit, 1967), p. 73 (hereafter cited as *DLG*).

4. Maurice Blanchot, *L'espace littéraire* (Paris: Gallimard, 1955); see Roland Barthes in *Sur Racine* and *Writing Degree Zero*.

5. In Jacques Derrida, *L'écriture et la différence* (Paris: Seuil, 1967) (hereafter cited as *ED*).

6. For a penetrating discussion of this point, see Marjorie Grene, "Life, Death, and Language: Some Thoughts on Wittgenstein and Derrida," *Philosophy In and Out of Europe* (Berkeley, Los Angeles, London: University of California Press, 1976), esp. p. 148.

7. Paul Ricoeur, "Qu'est-ce qu'un Texte? Expliquer et comprendre," in *Hermeneutik und Dialektik,* II (Tübingen: J. C. B. Mohr, 1970), 181-200 (hereafter cited as "QT").

8. Gadamer mentioned a similar distinction at a conference on hermeneutics in New York in December 1970 and at that time urged it upon Ricoeur, who also attended and spoke. More recently, in the new "Nachwort" to the third edition of *Wahrheit und Methode,* Gadamer also uses such a distinction in dealing with those literary texts that transcend their original historical context and speak to later historical times just as originally and contemporaneously (*WM* 538 ff.). Gadamer calls these texts "eminent texts," but he could have just as well spoken of them as "immanent." The latter term may have the disadvantage of suggesting that the work exists independently of its *Wirkungsgeschichte,* but the subsequent discussion will show that such an understanding of "immanence" does not necessarily follow. The term "eminent" has the disadvantage of not applying strictly to literary or poetic texts. (There are texts that are eminent because of their effects—for example, famous scientific formulas, political speeches, or peace treaties—but are not eminent literary texts.) Here the term "immanent" is preferred because it is the more common term in Anglo-American theory of literary criticism. It is used with the intention of keeping the discussion specific to literature, where a work's eminence is a function of the work rather than of some causal relation between the text and other events of another nature (such as political events).

9. Paul Ricoeur, "The Model of the Text: Meaningful Action Considered as a Text," *Social Research,* 38 (1971), 535.

10. In *Sein und Zeit* (see pp. 85-89) Heidegger contrasts the world (as the "wherein" [Worin] of man's understanding) with the worldhood of the world (the total disclosure, the *Woraufhin,* that gives particular entities within the world their meaning). The worldhood is not something that can be pointed to, as one can point to particular entities, but it is the whole that is presupposed in the very act of discerning the meaning or function of particular entities.

11. Paul Ricoeur, "La métaphore et le problème central de l'herméneutique," *Revue philosophique de Louvain* (February 1972), pp. 93-112.

12. Ricoeur, "The Model of the Text," pp. 544, 548, 549.

13. See G. W. F. Hegel, *The Logic of Hegel*, 2d ed., trans. W. Wallace (London: Oxford University Press, 1904 [1962]), pp. 26-28 (paragraphs 16 and 17).

14. See Barthes, *Critique et vérité*, pp. 56 ff.

15. Paul Ricoeur, "The Model of the Text," p. 554.

16. Cited by Gadamer, *WM* 344. "Axiom der Gewöhnlichkeit: Wie es bei uns steht und um uns ist, so muss es überall gewesen sein, denn das ist ja alles so natürlich."

17. This term will be referred to as "hermeneutic consciousness" or "hermeneutic awareness."

18. In a lecture given at Yale University and other places in the United States in 1968; cf. *WM* 153 ff., 367 f.

Four: Truth and Criticism

1. In Michael Hamburger's prose translation: "Yet us it behoves, you poets, to stand bare-headed beneath God's thunderstorms, to grasp the Father's ray, itself, with our own hands, and to offer the heavenly gift to the people, wrapped in our song." In *Hölderlin* (Baltimore: Penguin, 1961), pp. 79-80.

2. As E. D. Hirsch argues (see *VI*, Appendix II).

3. Oskar Becker, "Die Fragwürdigkeit der Transzendierung der ästhetischen Dimension der Kunst (im Hinblick auf den I. Teil von *Wahrheit und Methode*)," *Philosophische Rundschau*, 10 (1962), 232.

4. Franz Wieacker, "Notizen zur rechtshistorischen Hermeneutik," *Nachrichten der Akademie der Wissènschaften in Göttingen*, I. Philologisch-Historische Klasse, 1 (Jahrgang 1963), 9.

5. Helmut Kuhn, "Wahrheit und geschichtliches Verstehen. Bemerkungen zu H.-G. Gadamers philosophischer Hermeneutik," *Historische Zeitschrift*, 193, 2 (1961), 381.

6. Becker's critique is directly discussed in Gadamer's "Vorwort" to *WM* (see pp. XVI-XVII), where the aesthetic attitude is rejected on the grounds that its notion of a work-in-itself (Werk an sich) is too abstract.

7. Emilio Betti, *HMG*, pp. 43-44.

8. Karl-Otto Apel, "Szientismus oder transzendentale Hermeneutik?" in *Hermeneutik und Dialektik*, Vol. I, ed. R. Bubner et al (Tübingen: J. C. B. Mohr, 1970) (herewith cited as *HD* I).

9. See H.-G. Gadamer, "Replik," in *Hermeneutik und Ideologiekritik*, ed. K.-O. Apel et al. (Frankfurt: Suhrkamp, 1971), pp. 283-317 (hereafter cited as "R").

10. Hirsch argues that our knowledge of the work's meaning is conditioned by our preunderstanding of the genre of the work (see *VI* 236 f.). If the category of genre is a valid one under which to subsume artworks, it is at most *one way* to apply the hermeneutic concept of a tradition of interests or a community of interpretation.

11. Jürgen Habermas, *Zur Logik der Sozialwissenschaften,* Beiheft 5, *Philosophische Rundschau* (1967) (hereafter cited as *ZLS*); also available from Suhrkamp (Frankfurt, 1970), and in an English translation.

12. H.-G. Gadamer, "Rhetorik, Hermeneutik und Ideologiekritik," *Kleine Schriften,* I, 113-130 (hereafter cited as *KS* I).

13. Jürgen Habermas, *Erkenntnis und Interesse* (Frankfurt: Suhrkamp, 1968) (hereafter cited as *EI*).

14. Jürgen Habermas, "Der Universalitätsanspruch der Hermeneutik," in *Hermeneutik und Dialektik,* I, 73-103.

15. This anthology includes not only these texts from the exchange between Habermas and Gadamer but also those of other authors contributing to the *Hermeneutikstreit.*

16. See *Erkenntnis und Interesse,* chap. 2, 3.

17. Habermas, *EI* 358-359; quoted from the English translation, *Knowledge and Human Interests,* trans. Jeremy J. Shapiro (Boston: Beacon Press, 1971), p. 295.

18. Quoted by Habermas, *ZLS* 165 (Danto, p. 17).

19. Quoted by Habermas, *ZLS* 164 (Danto, p. 115).

20. Wolfhart Pannenberg, "Hermeneutik und Universalgeschichte," *Zeitschrift für Theologie und Kirche,* 60 (1963), 90-121. The translation is published in *History and Hermeneutic* (New York: Harper Torchbooks, 1967), but the page references to the German text are given here, as this book, which is out-of-print, includes the German pagination. Gadamer's own reply to Pannenberg (see *KS* I, 126-127) is not completely persuasive because it does not engage Pannenberg on the question of the objectifying assertion (Aussage).

21. Pannenberg writes: "Only a conception of the course of history which in fact links what is past to the present situation and its future horizon can form the comprehensive horizon within which the limited present horizon of the interpreter and the historical horizon of the text fuse, because only in that way, within that comprehensive horizon, are the past and the present preserved in their historical uniqueness and difference over against each other; they are preserved in such a way, nevertheless, that they enter as instances into the unity of a historical context that includes both" (ibid. 116). Pannenberg's statement has much to recommend it. It preserves the historical difference in a hermeneutic awareness in a way that a psychologistic concept of appropriation does not. To that extent Pannenberg and Gadamer are not widely divergent. Their disagreement is most fundamental on the question of the extent to which this overarching concept can be "universal" and explicit.

22. S. Freud, *Civilization and Its Discontents* (New York: W. W. Norton & Co., 1962), p. 91.

23. Ibid., p. 92; emphasis added.

Five: Hermes and Clio

1. Martin Heidegger, "Die Zeit des Weltbildes," *Holzwege,* 4th ed. (Frankfurt: Vittorio Klostermann, 1963), p. 76; available in a translation by Marjorie

Grene, "The Age of the World View," *Boundary 2,* vol. 4, no. 2 (1976).

2. Friedrich Nietzsche, "Vom Nutzen und Nachteil der Historie für das Leben," *Unzeitgemässe Betrachtungen, II,* in *Nietzsche Werke: Kritische Gesamtausgabe,* ed. G. Colli and M. Montinari, Vol. III, 1 (Berlin: Walter de Gruyter, 1972), 243 (hereafter cited as *UB*).

3. Paul de Man, *Blindness and Insight: Essays in the Rhetoric of Contemporary Criticism* (New York: Oxford University Press, 1971), especially p. 151.

4. See Friedrich Nietzsche, *On the Genealogy of Morals,* Essay III, Section 28.

5. Friedrich Nietzsche, *Werke,* 2d ed., ed. Karl Schlechta (Munich: Hanser, 1960), 3:486; cited by Jurgen Habermas, *Knowledge and Human Interests,* trans. Jeremy J. Shapiro (Boston: Beacon Press, 1971), p. 291.

6. There is one important qualification. Man is not totally free to break completely with the tradition in order to rethink it. The hermeneutic analysis emphasizes thought's entrenchment in the tradition. The limitations tradition imposes on thought keep thought from becoming totally conscious of the tradition as tradition. The point of the criticism of Nietzsche shows its importance here. If the past were completely different from the present, the past would indeed have to be totally opaque or totally transparent to the present. Thus, not being able to say anything truly about the past would come to much the same thing as being able to say anything at all about it. Hermeneutics suggests that present thought is itself still past thought to a certain extent. Gadamer follows Hölderlin in noting that the new is the truth of the old insofar as the new represents the fulfillment of possibilities conditioned by the old itself. This position is similar to one held by Merleau-Ponty (in his chapter on "Freedom" in the *Phenomenology of Perception*) and by Roland Barthes (in *Writing Degree Zero*). In critique of Sartre's concept of total freedom, they argue that at any one moment in history there is not really an infinity of possibilities, since the historical situation itself makes some possibilities more real than others. There is no reason to rule out an intermediate position between absolute freedom and absolute cultural determinism. One need not confuse cultural conditioning with unthinking acceptance of the standards and values of a given age.

7. Hans Robert Jauss, *Literaturgeschichte als Provokation* (Frankfurt: Suhrkamp, 1970), p. 216.

8. Emil Staiger, "The Questionable Nature of Value Problems," in *Problems of Literary Evaluation,* ed. Joseph Strelka (University Park: Pennsylvania State University Press, 1969). Staiger also tries to reconcile the interplay of the ideal and the historical by suggesting that they are involved in a necessary dialectic: "So it is necessary that the ideal in art perish continually, that fashion and taste, even barbarism, thrust aside perfection in style. For only those things that have declined and perished can celebrate a resurrection." He adds further, in Nietzschean language but with an un-Nietzschean conclusion: "Throughout history we find no doctrine that has been permanently acknowledged by all those whom it concerned. When man encounters that which does not advance him or support his self-affirmation, he tends either not to understand it or, if he does understand it, to forget it in the shortest possible order. This kind of misunderstanding or

forgetting is the normal relationship between the younger and older generations. The younger generation, of course, is continually asserting that it has overcome the older one, but often it can only say this because it is unaware of the older generation's achievements.'' These points are taken up in a more subtle way by Harold Bloom.

9. Michael Riffaterre, "Describing Poetic Structures: Two Approaches to Baudelaire's 'les Chats' " in *Structuralism,* ed. Jacques Ehrmann (Garden City, N.Y.: Doubleday Anchor Books, 1970), pp. 188-230 (hereafter cited as "DPS"). See Roman Jakobson and Claude Lévi-Strauss, " 'Les Chats' de Charles Baudelaire," *L'Homme,* 2 (1962), 5-21.

10. Published in Stanley Fish, *Self-Consuming Artifacts: The Experience of Seventeenth-Century Literature* (Berkeley, Los Angeles, London: University of California Press, 1972), pp. 383-426 (hereafter cited as "LR").

11. *The Verbal Icon,* p. 21.

12. Ibid., p. 34; quoted by Fish, p. 400.

13. The essential difference between Fish's informed reader and Riffaterre's superreader is that the latter concept presupposes a notion of style as stress and limits itself to oppositions and contrasts. Fish is opposed to the distinction between linguistic facts and stylistic facts, i.e., between meaning and style (and he correctly observes that he should be willing to discard the very terms "meaning" and "style"). His stylistics thus would not need supplementation by other philological methods (see pp. 424-425).

14. Gadamer's notion of *Wirkungsgeschichte* is certainly not paradoxical in this way. Any reading is itself conditioned by a tradition of prior readings, including ones contemporaneous with the production of the text. The relation between these readings and one another, as between the readings and the text, is mediated by a common interest in the *Sache.*

15. Harold Bloom, *The Anxiety of Influence: A Theory of Poetry* (New York: Oxford University Press, 1973) (hereafter cited as *AI*).

16. Ibid., pp. 63-64. Bloom does not specify why the Oedipal rivalry rather than, say, the Electra situation becomes the paradigm for the analysis of poetry, but the appeal to Freud is in any case only indirect since Bloom claims that the reading of poetry is not in any relevant way the result of the sublimation of sex, but only of the sublimation of aggression (*AI* 115).

17. Richard Rorty's review appears in the *Princeton Alumni Magazine,* 66 (Fall 1975), 17.

18. Gadamer extends this point to poetic evaluation when he notes, "All criticism of poetry, as long as it does not say that the supposed poetry is not really poetry because it fails in its 'realization,' is therefore always self-criticism of the interpretation" (*KS* II 185).

Index